THE MANX TEMPEST

*For Barbara
With very best
from Paul*

Published by
Digital Print Media Ltd
www.printandpublish.co.uk

All rights reserved.

No part of this book may be reproduced in any form by photocopying or
any electronic or mechanical means, including information storage or retrieval systems,
without permissions in writing from both the copyright owner and the publisher of the book.

First Edition published 2014
© Paul Robertshaw 2014

Printed and bound in Great Britain by
Digital Print Media Ltd

A catalogue record for this book
is available from The British Library
ISBN 978-1-910090-07-7

Introduction

I had known for a while that there was a gap, a seven year gap, in Shakespeare's adult biography and that this started after he had moved from Stratford-on-Avon to London. I also knew that this period precedes the production of any of his plays. I am no student of Shakespeare, but have always had an interest in the man. For example I have no difficulty in accepting degrees of collaboration in his work; for me as a former academic lawyer, *The Merchant of Venice* is a prime example. However I took exception to that scurrilous and snobbish film *Anonymous* which made out that he was an ignorant provincial dolt who could not (rather than would not) sign his name (for obvious security reasons). I also knew that although the Civil War had destroyed any documentary evidence, there has always been folkloric support for his sheltering in Lancashire from dangerous politics in London; there is respectable academic support for the Lancashire theory.

It slowly dawned on me that if Shakespeare was doing the rounds of tutoring the recusant gentry's children in Lancashire, he might well have ended up, with good reports, at Knowsley, the seat of the Stanleys, Earls of Derby. As a Manxman that made me sit up and take notice, since the Stanleys were the feudal Lords of Mann, the Isle of Man, some eighty miles sea passage from Knowsley through Liverpool. If you are going to have a feudal regime on your island –as was the case for many centuries- the Stanleys were about as good as you could get. Apart from their respect for the Island's ancient institutions (the Tynwald legislature based on Viking sheading 'constituencies', Captains of Parishes, the citizen's right to Petition of Doleance, and Deemster judges), they largely overcame the absenteeism problem by instituting a Stewardship with permanent residence of the Manx Gaelic speaking (originally Lancashire) Radcliffe family.

Actually my imagination did *not* get Shakespeare onto the Island just like that. The artistic penny did not drop immediately. It followed on from the idea of the Isle of Man being the site of *The Tempest*. How many people know that Lawrence Durrell in 1938 toyed with the idea of a Greek Corfu based Tempest?

Once I had mentally transported Shakespeare to the Island with the Earl on an annual visitation to establish the Derby horse race, the practical issues of writing began to fall into place:

The Earl arranges for Steward Daniel Radcliffe to show the visitor Shakespeare around on foot for a few days, in pursuing the Earl's and his own business. In so doing they encounter a variety of monoglot and illiterate Manx characters, with Daniel Radcliffe acting as interpreter. These characters, including Steward Radcliffe, in turn morph into characters in *The Tempest*:

Steward Radcliffe as Ferdinand
The Healer Simon Callow (another Manx surname) as Prospero
Danny 'the Moo' Callinan, a tenant farmer of the Earl, as Caliban
Joni Joughin (Helena Bonham-Carter) a knitter, as Sycorax
'Young' and 'Old' Jago, rabitters and distillers, as Stephano and Trinculo.
Ferdinand re-morphs as Steward Radcliffe to introduce the two Jagos before continuing as Ferdinand to the conclusion of *The Tempest*.

This double-casting is part of the great Bollywood tradition which I am pleased to acknowledge, and the film has other Bollywood features. The fractured narratives which do this by interleaving the Manx walking tour and *The Tempest* are not novel in the cinema- a sophisticated contemporary example is *The Cloud Atlas*. I am grateful to Hilary Dugdale, then of Isle of Man Film, for pushing me towards this mode; it raises the script from 'novel' to proper cinematic form. I must also acknowledge here the generous time of Brian Stowell, secretary of Yn Cheshaght Ghailckagh, who made almost all of the Manx Gaelic translation, which Steward Radcliffe interprets to Shakespeare. It was a pleasant surprise encountering enthusiastic Manxman John Clucas at Digital Print Media; my thanks to him too.

Beyond Hilary's initial mentoring I have had to learn to swim at the deep end where funding and production of the film were concerned; Isle of Man Film has no funds today and is now a servicing company for film production on the Island. I have learned a bit about the film industry during the year, not all of it comfortable! However it has not been entirely gloomy as I have had the privilege and pleasure of the respective agents of Helena Bonham-Carter, Simon Callow and Daniel Radcliffe granting 'green–light' status for their clients. Sadly my attempt to extend this to the Manx songbird Samantha Barks after her outstanding performance in *Les Miserables* did not get past her agent. Here is the vignette part I wrote for her:

'RADCLIFFE APPROACHES ONE OF THOSE WAITING (for the Healer Callow), A YOUNG WOMAN HOLDING TWO NANNY GOATS ON LEATHER LEADS.
RADCLIFFE (in Manx Gaelic)
I believe you are the daughter of Tom Quine, the boat-builder of Laxey
KITTY QUINE
That is so Steward Daniel. I am walked here with my goats because their milk is foul to the tongue, although it makes cheese good enough
RADCLIFFE
Master Callow will certainly help you. Good Day to you and your family
KITTY QUINE
Then I am blessed. Good Day to you Steward David
RADCLIFFE TO SHAKESPEARE
Her goats produce bad milk but good cheese. My guess is that the sage will warn her to keep them off the seastrand. The sea-wrack they eat there makes for tasty meat but can corrupt the milk'.........

At the end of the day one has to face up to the colossal costs involved in film-making and that despite the obvious pressures to dumb down, worthwhile films, popular as well as 'art-house', do still emerge as a triumph for collective artistic talent and tenacity. Film is the great art form of the twentieth century, and maybe of the twenty-first as well.

Finally members of my family have helped me with my tendency towards computerexia; my children Anna and Rory and my granddaughter Julia. I thank them all and can express here my appreciation of their tolerance of my eccentric propensities.

Paul Robertshaw November 2013

THE MANX TEMPEST

> *Copyright Paul Robertshaw*
> *2013*

Log-line:

Shakespeare's mystery solved.
Why did Shakespeare disappear for 7 years?
Where? What to do?
Did this impact any of his plays?
Now find out

GENRE:

Biopic. Shakespeare Drama.

TONE:

Romantic Fantasy

TARGET AUDIENCES:

12A; All ages and genders
World-wide Anglophone audiences
There is implicit focus on the large Indian
market
Aimed at popular cinema chains and not limited to
art-house venues.

EFFECT ON AUDIENCES:

* Enlarging our view of Shakespeare as person and
playwright
* Showing how a writer's experience alchemically
transmutes into dramatic personalities and action
* Enjoying The Manx Tempest with catchy music and
beautiful Manx locations.

THE FILM'S MESSAGES:

* There's more to Shakespeare than we thought
* Love-At-First-Sight can triumph
* Wrongs can be righted
* Retirement can be painful
* Hidden Message: Caliban gets his Island back!

SYNOPSIS:
The Manx Tempest is structured around two inter-
related narratives: an event in a 7 year chapter of
Shakespeare's life, and one play that eventually
emerged from it: *The Tempest.* The two narratives are
bound together by the use of 'Bollywood' double-
casting: Helena Bonham-Carter (green-lit) as Joni
Joughin, a knitter on the Isle of Man **and** as the
witch Sycorax (inset -as Sycorax does not appear in
The Tempest); Simon Callow (green-lit) as the Healer
SC **and** as Prospero; Daniel Radcliffe (green-lit) as
the Earl of Derby's Manx Steward DR **and** as
Ferdinand. Also (uncast) Bridie Callow, the Healer's
daughter **and** as Miranda; Danny 'the Moo' Callinan, a
farmer, **and** as Caliban; also the Old and Young
Jagos, rabitters/distillers **and** as Stephano and
Trinculo.

1. Shakespeare is advised to flee London. He does
so, laying a false trail for the secret police.
2. WS has tutored for the gentry in Lancashire and
arrived at the Earl of Derby, feudal Lord of the
Isle of Man. He invites WS to join him on a voyage
to his island.
III (ActI Sc.1 *The Tempest*) A Storm at Sea
4. Derby's Steward DR offers to show WS around
interpret.
5. They visit 'Wiseman'/Hypnotist/Healer Simon
Callow. Shakespeare is impressed by Callow.
Radcliffe is impressed by Callow's daughter, Bridie
Callow.
VI Prospero (*SC transmuted*) and his daughter Miranda
(*BC transmuted*) discuss their fate. Ariel
introduced; 'he' is the creative essence of Prospero
[ie WS].
7. The knitter Joni Joughin (H B-C) ignores DR and
WS.
VIII Prospero threatens Ariel who is chafing for
freedom, and reminds 'him' that he was freed from
torture by the witch Sycorax (*H B-C/Joni Joughin
transmuted- inset*)
9. Radcliffe deals with Danny 'the Moo' Callinan, a
farmer.
10. Prospero again threatens Ariel. Miranda wakens
from a trance induced by Prospero. Caliban (*D'The
Moo'C transmuted*) has foul relations with Prospero
and Miranda. Ferdinand (*DR transmuted*) is brought in
by Ariel. For Ferdinand and Miranda it's love at
first sight. Prospero disrupts them by hypnosis.
11. The shipwrecked courtiers on the island. Ariel
disrupts.
12. DR (*re-transmuted*) and WS encounter Old and

Young Jago, rabitters and maybe distillers
13. Caliban is encountered by Stephano and Trinculo (*The Jagos transmuted*)-slapstick, drunken humour.
14-19. *The Tempest* concludes with justice for Prospero and forgiveness for the usurper Alonso. Ferdinand and Miranda are to cement this with their marriage. There is a sub-plot: Caliban and his new friends plot to murder Prospero; Ariel disrupts again by diverting them with a comic dressing up scene. The mariners arrive safely to take all back to Naples. Prospero makes his Farewell speech.

CONTACT: PaulRobertshaw710@btinternet.com

SCREEN TEXT:

William Shakespeare did not commence his
theatrical career in London as a playwright, but
as an actor and poet, then as actor-manager. He
had important patrons, including Edward de Vere,
Earl of Oxford, who was also a collaborator and
friend. These were turbulent times, exemplified
by the imprisonment and later execution of the
Queen's Catholic cousin Mary, Queen of Scots;
also the unsuccessful Spanish and English
Armadas, 1588-89. Shakespeare was threatened by
these tensions as at least one of his parents was
a Catholic. What is clear is that there are seven
'missing' years from his adult life, 1585-1592
when he disappeared. To this day there remain no
records of his actions or whereabouts. There are
two speculations as to what happened:

                                        FADES

                    SCREEN TEXT

The year 1585. It is DAYTIME. A room on the upper
floor of a house in London, occupied by William
Shakespeare.

                                        FADES
Street noises can be heard

The shutters of the unglazed windows are open.
Shakespeare is sitting at a table by the window.
There are sheets of parchment on the table and an
ink-pot.
He holds a quill pen.

There is a gentle knock at the door.

Shakespeare puts down his quill, rises, crosses
the room and opens the door.

ENTER Edward de Vere, Earl of Oxford

                    SHAKESPEARE

        My Lord Oxford I am as
        pleased as I am
        surprised to see you
        here.

OXFORD

Will

The two men embrace warmly.

OXFORD (CONT'D)

I come on urgent
business and reached
your abode by a crooked
route to avoid the
chance of being
followed.

SHAKESPEARE

My Lord I am grieved to
hear of any danger you
may face

OXFORD

It is not I but you Will
who is endangered

SHAKESPEARE

How so my Lord?

OXFORD

Yester-eve I was at
Court to attend the new
Masque. There, a friend,
whom I name not, and who
is close to the Queen's
Council, warned me that
Walsingham,
the Queen's master of
spiery
and intelligencer, has
decided that our
theatrical ventures are
seditious. As we know
the Puritan party that
he represents is no
friend of dramatics. The
advice was for me to
return to the country
and keep away from
London: to keep my head
by keeping it down. As

for you Will, you are
the goat to be 'scaped:

Oxford mockingly mimes 'Arrest','Ordeal'; and
'Hanging':

Arrest is certain; The
Tower is likely; Ordeal
probable; a public
Hanging possible. So the
scaped must 'scape. A
London jury might save
you from conviction; but
you would still face the
ecclesiastical
authorities, where no
jury sits and where
evidence can be taken
from you by public
examination in the
courtroom.

SHAKESPEARE

Why should I be in
danger from the Church's
court?

OXFORD

Will, as I am thy friend
and here for thy safety,
do not parry me with
smart wordplay. It is no
secret that you love and
lust after that
blackamoor 'the Strumpet
of Clerkenewell'. I have
read your verses to your
'dark lady'.

SHAKESPEARE

Love I freely admit, but
dalliance I deny.

OXFORD

Be that as it may, your
denial will not get you
far in that court.
Our Lord would support
your love -indeed rumour

has it that he married a
whore. But he clearly
opposed adultery. Your
dark lady is, as you
well know, married to
the keeper of a
notorious stew, and
adultery is adultery
even against a cuckolded
brothel keeper. Worse:
you and I know too much
of another crime. So do
my [He winks at WS]
fears deceive me that
its name we durs't not
utter? The court has
punishments worse than
hanging for such crimes.

                    SHAKESPEARE

Pacing the floor
          Where can I go but to
          Stratford, where enemies
          would soon find me.
          I am undone.

          OXFORD

          I came here with a
          solution for you. Here
          is a letter of
          introduction to a
          relative of mine, a
          catholic gentleman of
          the County Palatine.

Oxford hands Shakespeare a sealed letter
          It is not as far as
          Scotland but it is
          safer. You will tutor
          his family in return for
          shelter. There are many
          such recusants in
          Lancashire, so in time
          you may tutor others.
          They have good
          libraries, so you will
          not starve. You must not
          return until you have
          word from me. You must
          part forthwith and

without farewells.

                    SHAKESPEARE

I will take but two
satchels and will myself
take a crooked way to
The Angel, where I will
buy a walking nag to
proceed -with your
lordship's consent- to
Stratford to say
farewell to my wife and
to make arrangements for
her comfort in my
absence.

                    OXFORD

Aye, but enter after
dark and leave the next
morning before dawn.
There can be no
lingering, nor dallying.

                    SHAKESPEARE

I will leave the nag for
her disposal and take
the covered wagon to
Coventry, where I will
purchase another walking
nag to continue my
journey.

                    OXFORD

This is the best we can
hope for in these
troubled times.

                    SHAKESPEARE [strocking his chin]

I have a sudden
stratagem for you to
consider if it may
please you

                    OXFORD

Speak on Will

SHAKESPEARE

If t'were possible for
you to arrange for a
person in your trust to
be at The Tabard
tonight. Kit will be
there.

OXFORD

Kit Marlowe, thy rival
and well known to be in
Walsingham's pay and
pocket.

SHAKESPEARE

The self-same Kit. He
must overhear that I am
run away and may serve
the Queen's enemies in
Flanders and that I
shall depart from one of
the Cinque ports -he
knows not which. By this
means shall the Queen's
agents rush to the
South-East, whilst Will
the wily bard will have
flown to the North-West.

OXFORD

A brave stratagem. It
shall be done. And now
dear Will we must part.
Farewell and Adieu.

They embrace again.

EXIT OXFORD

FADE OUT.

SCREEN TEXT

It is 1589. Shakespeare has been in exile in
Lancashire for three years. He has acted as tutor
to the children of several prominent local
families and moved to Knowsley Hall, seat of the
greatest of them, the Stanleys, Kingmakers of the

Tudor Dynasty, Earls of Derby, and feudal Lords
of The Isle of Mann.

SCREEN TEXT and SCENE

An oak-panelled room in Knowsley Hall.
Shakespeare attends the Earl of Derby who is
seated at a large table.

DERBY

Master Shakespeare I
receive good reports of
your learning and its
exposition from my son.
Indeed you came to my
seat after I had
received such good
reports from my
neighbours and friends
whom you have previously
served.

SHAKESPEARE

My Lord, both you and
your friends have given
me shelter, and beyond
that, refuge from a
grievous fate, so it
behoves me to respond
with my best endeavours.
I am pleased that your
children give a good
report of me and I hope
to continue to be worthy
of it and them.

DERBY

I called you here for
another reason, which I
trust will interest you.
You have expressed your
sadness at the loss of
two Spanish galleons on
my domain, the Isle of
Man in the terrible
tempest that attended
the Spanish king's
invasion Armada. The

galleon Aragon foundered
on the rocks of the
South-East of the Isle.
There was never any hope
for her or her crew: God
rest their souls. The
Minorca fared better,
breaking up by the
fishing village of
Laxey, where some of her
crew were saved and are
now cared for there.

SHAKESPEARE

It was a providential
deliverance.

DERBY [rising]

It is my purpose to make
a visitation to my
domain of Mann each
year. Alas, that cannot
always be done, but I
will do so this year,
indeed next month. I
have however a trusty
family of Stewards to
carry on my business at
all times by residing in
permanence on the
island.
This family of Radcliffe
-originating here-
manage my business well
and rule with a fair
hand, which I encourage.
They all speak the
language of the Manx
which much eases their
tasks. I am inviting you
to take passage with me
and when, God willing,
we make landfall I will
place you in the care of
the young Steward Daniel
Radcliffe, who will take
you about with him on
his business, when you
may observe the
character and customs of

these my subjects.
For myself, I have
business to attend with
greater persons of the
island, land Captains of
Parishes and
representatives in the
ancient assembly of
Tynwald. My business
principally is to
establish on the island
an annual Derby prize
race without fences, for
the finest horses. Also,
Tynwald has passed to me
a Petition of Doleance
from farmers of the
Parish of Ballaugh, who
are aggrieved by
Nature's enlargement of
the willow bogs in that
part;

Turning over plans on the table
they aver that soon they
will have no grazing
land for their livestock
and seek the digging of
a drain to the sea three
miles away.
This would be a great
enterprise requiring the
coming together of men
from four parishes over
some years. I doubt I
can support this at this
time.
This business will take
at most five days, when
we will return.

SHAKESPEARE

My Lord I am as ever
beholden to you.

DERBY

I believe you have a yen
for travel, having
risked your vacation
last year travelling to

Scotland and its capital
city.

SHAKESPEARE

Brave or foolhardy, I
know not which, but your
lordship will understand
that experience is the
food of the playwright
and one day, God
willing, that craft may
be opened to me. I may
return to Scotland if my
duties so allow.

DERBY

We share your hopes.
Meanwhile we shall sail
for a day on my barque
on the first tide of the
first Monday of the
month coming, so prepare
yourself- my confessor
is available for you. I
put great trust in the
skill and experience of
Manx sea captains. One
not only trusts them;
under the law of the sea
they have absolute
command and demand of
all aboard their vessel
-even kings must obey
them and their agents
when aboard.
Captain Maddrell, who is
well known to me advises
that no human soul is
mightier than the ocean.
Any who say other risk
an early drowning.

SHAKESPEARE

My Lord, I shall prepare
myself accordingly

Shakespeare bows and EXITS

FADE OUT

On a ship at sea: a tempestuous noise; of thunder
and lightning heard. [Spanish Head, Isle of Man
occasionally visible]

ENTER a master and a boatswain

MASTER

Boatswain!

BOATSWAIN

Here, master: what
cheer?

MASTER

Good, speak to the
mariners:
fall to't, yarely, or we
run ourselves aground:
bestir, bestir.

EXIT

BOATSWAIN

Heigh, my hearts!
Cheerly, cheerly, my
hearts!
Yare, yare! Take in the
topsail. Tend to the
master's whistle.
Blow, till thou burst
thy wind,
if room enough!
     [Bosun's whistle heard]

ENTER Mariners to work the rigging

ENTER Alonso, Sebastian, Antonio, Ferdinand,
Gonzalo, and others
(The courtiers are dressed in cutaway tailed
coats and long waistcoats, with Asian
fabrics -a kaleidoscope of colour for these
popinjays)

ALONSO

Good boatswain, have
care.
Where's the master?
Play the men.

BOATSWAIN

I pray now, keep below.

ANTONIO

Where is the master,
boatswain?

BOATSWAIN

Do you not hear him?
You mar our labour:
keep your cabins:
you do assist the storm.

GONZALO

Nay, good, be patient.

BOATSWAIN

When the sea is. Hence!
What cares these roarers
for the name of king?
To cabin: Silence!
Trouble us not.

GONZALO

Good, yet remember whom
thou hast aboard.

BOATSWAIN

None that I more love
than myself. You are a
counsellor; if you can
command these elements
to silence, and work the
peace of the present, we
will not hand a rope
more;
use your authority: if
you cannot, give thanks
you have lived so long,
and make yourself ready
in your cabin for the
mischance of the hour,
if it so hap.
Cheerly, good hearts!
Out of our way, I say.

EXIT.

GONZALO

I have great comfort
from this fellow:
methinks he hath no
drowning mark upon him;
his complexion is
perfect gallows. Stand
fast, good fate, to his
hanging: make the rope
of his destiny our
cable,
for our own doth little
advantage.
If he be not born to be
hanged,
our case is miserable.

EXEUNT

RE-ENTER the Boatswain

BOATSWAIN

Down with the topmast!
Yare! Lower, lower!
Bring her to try with
main-course.

(A cry within)

A plague upon this
howling!
They're louder than the
weather
or our office.

RE-ENTER Sebastian, Antonio, and Gonzalo

Yet again! What do you
here?
Shall we give o'er and
drown?
Have you a mind to sink?

SEBASTIAN

A pox o' your throat,
you bawling,

blasphemous,
incharitable dog!

BOATSWAIN

Work you then.

ANTONIO

Hang, cur! Hang, you
whoreson, insolent
noisemaker!
We are less afraid to be
drowned than thou art.

GONZALO

I'll warrant him for
drowning; though the
ship were no stronger
than a nutshell and as
leaky
as an unstanched wench.

BOATSWAIN

Lay her a-hold, a-hold!
Set her two courses off
to sea again; lay her
off.

ENTER Mariners wet

MARINERS

All lost! To prayers, to
prayers! All lost!

BOATSWAIN

What, must our mouths be
cold?

GONZALO

The king and prince at
prayers! Let's assist
them,
for our case is as
theirs.

SEBASTIAN

I'm out of patience.

ANTONIO

We are merely cheated of
our lives by drunkards:
this wide-chapp'd
rascal--would thou
might'st lie drowning
the washing of ten
tides!

GONZALO

He'll be hang'd yet,
though every drop of
water swear against it
and gape at widest to
glut him.

        (A confused
         noise within:
         'mercy on
         us!'-- 'we
         split, we
         split!'--
         'farewell, my
         wife and
         children!'--
         'farewell,
         brother!'--'we
         split, we
         split, we
         split!')

ANTONIO

Let's all sink with the
king.

SEBASTIAN

Let's take leave of him.

EXEUNT Antonio and Sebastian

GONZALO

Now would I give a
thousand furlongs of sea
for an acre

of barren ground, long
heath, brown furze,
anything.
The wills above be done!
But I would fain die a
dry death.

                              EXEUNT.
                              FADES

On the Isle of Man. DAY. Outside a dwelling.
Daniel Radcliffe, Lord DERBY's Steward is with
Shakespeare.

                    RADCLIFFE

          Master Shakespeare I
          trust that after last
          night's sleep your
          stomach has ceased its
          sea heaving; and that
          your belly is more
          composed so that you may
          proceed on your way with
          me?

                    SHAKESPEARE

          I thank you Steward
          Radcliffe.
          My spirits are again in
          balance
          and the excess of bile
          is now expurgated. I
          confess I have not seen
          such raw nature before.
          The surge and sway of
          the sea
          hath much perturb-ed me.

                    RADCLIFFE

          We can then proceed, and
          every step will refresh
          your spirits. From Lord
          Stanley I am instructed
          to take you in my
          company about his
          lordship's business
          these few days. That
          will be my pleasure as
          much as my duty. We

>   receive few visitors
>   from across. We will
>   sojourn nights with a
>   tenant of Lord Stanley.
>   The place is simple but
>   the care is good as are
>   the victuals and the
>   home-brewed jough.
>   On this island it is
>   usual to walk, often for
>   a distance. They say
>   here that God gave
>   Stanley three legs for
>   his arms, but we have
>   but two of each, so we
>   must practice them. So
>   we will walk, the best
>   of which is being close
>   to the country and its
>   folk. To ease this I
>   make you a gift of what
>   all wear, a pair of
>   carranes.

Radcliffe hands Shakespeare boots of in-turned
cowhide

>   And wool for your
>   greater comfort

Radcliffe hands Shakespeare two lumps of ginger
wool

Shakespeare stuffs and pulls on the carranes,
cross-laces them and then puts his feet in crude
wooden sabots.

>   I have some calls to
>   make which I pray may
>   interest you. One knows
>   not whom we may chance
>   upon on our journey. Our
>   first visit is not far
>   from here, where I have
>   business of mine own.

                         SHAKESPEARE

>   Let us depart. My
>   appetite for encounter
>   is awakened.

EXEUNT Radcliffe and Shakespeare up a track

FADES

Where several tracks converge is a well
maintained house with outbuildings. There are
people waiting outside, some with their sick on
carts, some with livestock.

RADCLIFFE

This is the home of
Simon Callow, one of the
respected Wise-Men and
Women healers of the
island.
The origins of this
tradition
we know not but it may
have been fifteen
centuries ago when the
Romans massacred the
Druid priests on the
island of Anglesey.
Any who escaped are
likely to have made for
the nearest land across
the sea. That is here.
Also some of the monks
pensioned off from our
Rushen Abbey on its
dissolution were skilled
herbalists and may have
passed on their
knowledge. Simon Callow
is typical of these
healers in that he
treats both persons and
beasts. He does not
usually treat women,
whom he recommends to
Fenella Farragher in the
next parish, or for
lumbago to Annie Corteen
in the parish of
Maughold. For bone-
setting of persons or
beasts, Orry Quayle of
Sulby has no equal.

Radcliffe and Shakespeare enter the house with
its *chiollagh* hearth in the centre of the floor.

The house is full of jars and bottles of preparations, with herbs hanging to dry from roof rafters. A patient is sitting in a chair, hypnotised, and repeating charm phrases in Manx Gaelic. Callow is attended by his daughter Bridie, who is beautiful despite her demure dress and carranes. It is evident that Radcliffe has eyes for her.

Radcliffe introduces Shakespeare to Callow, an imposing figure

> RADCLIFFE to Callow
>
> *{MANX GAELIC} Shoh fer-ynsee yn Chiarn Stanlagh ta cur shilley as y chiarn ayns mannin dellal rish cooishyn Tinval:*[Subtitles?] This is Lord Stanley's tutor who is visiting whilst his lordship is here on Tynwald business]

Callow and Shakespeare shake hands

> CALLOW gesturing to the

patient

> *Ta mee er chur y fer shoh ny chadley as t'eh gra oalyssu harrish dy chur shee-aigney da as dy chur jerrey er ny teamyn-tappey echey*

Radcliffe translates to Shakespeare
> This man I have put to sleep and in his trance he repeats charms to bring him peace of mind and to end his outbursts of temper

Callow wakens the patient *counting from Ten to One:*

Jeih, Nuy, Hooght, Shiaght, Shey, Queig, Kiare, Tree, Daa, Nane

> BRIDIE CALLOW to the

                    patient

          Yuan vel oo gennaghty ec
          shee nish

RADCLIFFE translates to SHAKESPEARE
          Juan do you feel at
          peace now

Juan nods and smiles

Bridie picks up and hands to Juan:

                    BRIDIE

          Shoh doss dy lus lheeah
          as druight ny marrey son
          dty chooislag dy chur
          dhyt dreamalyn millish
          Yuan

RADCLIFFE translates to Shakespeare
          Here is a bunch of
          lavender and rosemary
          for thy pillow to give
          thee sweet dreams Juan

Juan expresses thanks and EXITS

                    RADCLIFFE [to Callow]

          Ta sharragh woirryn aym
          nagh vel gientyn ga dy
          vel y collagh prowit. Ta
          mee geearree cur lhiam
          ee tra higym dys shoh
          reesht ayns mee dy hraa

RADCLIFFE translates to Shakespeare
          I have a filly who
          conceives not despite
          the stallion being
          proven. I wish to bring
          her on my next visit in
          a month's time

                    CALLOW

          Bare eh ac traa yn eayst
          noa

RADCLIFFE translates to Shakespeare

It would be best at the
time of the new moon

CALLOW

*Veoir Daniel by vie
lhiam tooilley skeddanyn
jaaghit veih'n thie-
jaagh ayns Purt ny h-
Inshey goll roosyn hug
shiu dou roie*

RADCLIFFE translates to Shakespeare
Steward Daniel I would
like some more kippers
from the smokehouse at
Peel, such as you
brought me on a previous
visit

RADCLIFFE to Callow

*Son shickrys shirrim daa
phiyr yeig diu S'mie
lhiams ad neesht*

RADCLIFFE translates to Shakespeare
I will certainly look
for a dozen pairs for
you. I also have a taste
for them.

RADCLIFFE [to Callow and
Bridie]

*Slane eu Simon as slane
eu Vreeshy. Ta mee
jeeaghyn roym d'akin
shiu reesht*
[Farewell Simon and
farewell to thee Bridie.
I look forward to our
next meeting]

CALLOW to Shakespeare

*Ta mee treishteil dy bee
yn shilley eu er yn
ellan ain foaysagh as dy
jig shiu dys shoh reesht
tra vees ny currymin eu
lowal da shen*

RADCLIFFE translates to Shakespeare
          I hope your visit to our
          island is fruitful and
          that you return when
          your duties permit

Shakespeare shakes Callow's hand

Bridie smiles

Outside Callow's door

                    SHAKESPEARE to Radcliffe

          Here is a mysterious
          medicine,
          me-thinks of much power.

                    RADCLIFFE

          Its power lies in
          physician and patient
          sharing their belief in
          it. The other side of
          this coin, which we are
          watchful of, are the
          dark arts in which one
          holds power over others.
          It is much troubling
          Lancashire at the
          present time.

                    SHAKESPEARE

          I hear of it everywhere.
          There would be less bad
          magic if there were wise
          healers as are evident
          here

                    RADCLIFFE

          Make no mistake they are
          two sides of the same
          coin.

Radcliffe and Shakespeare depart

                              FADES

The island. Before Prospero's cell.

ENTER {Simon Callow}Prospero and {Bridie
Callow}Miranda

                    MIRANDA

          If by your art, my
          dearest father, you have
          put the wild waters
          in this roar, allay
          them.
          The sky, it seems, would
          pour down stinking
          pitch, but that the sea,
          mounting to the welkin's
          cheek,
          dashes the fire out.

Miranda moves about

          O, I have suffered with
          those
          that I saw suffer:
          a brave vessel, who had,
          no doubt, some noble
          creature in her, dash'd
          all to pieces.
          O, the cry did knock
          against my very heart.
          Poor souls, they
          perish'd.
          Had I been any god of
          power,
          I would have sunk the
          sea within the earth or
          ere it should the good
          ship so have swallow'd
          and the fraughting souls
          within her.

                    PROSPERO

          Be collected:
          no more amazement:
          Tell your piteous heart
          there's no harm done.

                    MIRANDA

          O, woe the day!

                    PROSPERO

No harm.
I have done nothing but
in care of thee, of
thee, my dear one, thee,
my daughter, who art
ignorant of what thou
art, nought knowing of
whence I am, nor that I
am more better than
Prospero, master of a
full poor cell, and thy
no greater father.

                    MIRANDA

    More to know did never
    meddle with my thoughts.

Miranda sits

                    PROSPERO

    'tis time I should
    inform thee farther.
    Lend thy hand,
    and pluck my magic
    garment from me. So:

Prospero lays down his mantle

    Lie there, my art.
    Wipe thou thine eyes;
    have comfort.
    The direful spectacle of
    the wreck, which touch'd
    the very virtue of
    compassion in thee,
    I have with such
    provision in mine art so
    safely ordered that
    there is no soul--no,
    not so much perdition as
    an hair betid to any
    creature in the vessel
    which thou heard'st cry,
    which thou saw'st sink.
    Sit down;
    for thou must now know
    farther.

                    MIRANDA

You have often begun to
tell me what I am, but
stopp'd and left me to a
bootless inquisition,
concluding 'stay: not
yet.'

PROSPERO

The hour's now come;
the very minute bids
thee ope thine ear; obey
and be attentive.
Canst thou remember a
time before we came unto
this cell?
I do not think thou
canst, for then thou
wast not out three years
old.

MIRANDA

Certainly, sir, I can.

PROSPERO

By what? By any other
house or person?
Of any thing the image
tell me that hath kept
with thy remembrance.

MIRANDA

'tis far off
and rather like a dream
than an assurance that
my remembrance warrants.
Had I not four or five
women once that tended
me?

PROSPERO

Thou hadst, and more,
Miranda.
But how is it that this
lives in thy mind?
What seest thou else in
the dark backward and

abysm of time?
If thou remember'st
aught ere thou camest
here, how thou camest
here thou mayst.

MIRANDA

But that I do not.

PROSPERO

Twelve year since,
Miranda,
Twelve year since,
thy father was the Duke
of Milan and a prince of
power.

MIRANDA

Sir, are not you my
father?

PROSPERO

Thy mother was a piece
of virtue, and she said
thou
wast my daughter; and
thy father was Duke of
Milan;
and thou his only heir
and princess no worse
issued.

MIRANDA standing again

O the heavens!
What foul play had we,
That we came from
thence?
Or blessed was't we did?

PROSPERO

Both, both, my girl:
by foul play, as thou
say'st,
were we heaved thence,
but blessedly holp
hither.

MIRANDA

O, my heart bleeds
to think o' the teen
that I have turn'd you
to,
which is from my
remembrance! Please you,
farther.

PROSPERO

My brother and thy
uncle,
call'd Antonio--
I pray thee, mark me--
that a brother should be
so perfidious!--he whom
next thyself
of all the world I loved
and to him put
the manage of my state;
as at that time through
all the signories it was
the first and Prospero
the prime duke, being so
reputed
in dignity, and for the
liberal arts without a
parallel;
those being all my
study,
the government I cast
upon my brother and to
my state grew stranger,
being transported
and rapt in secret
studies.
Thy false uncle--
dost thou attend me?

MIRANDA

Sir, most heedfully.

PROSPERO

Being once perfected how
to grant suits, how to
deny them,
who to advance and who
to trash for over-

topping,
new created the
creatures that were
mine, I say, or changed
'em,
or else new form'd 'em;
having both the key
of officer and office,
set all hearts i' the
state
to what tune pleased his
ear;
that now he was the ivy
which had hid my
princely trunk,
and suck'd my verdure
out on't. Thou attend'st
not.

MIRANDA

O, good sir, I do

PROSPERO

I pray thee, mark me
I thus neglecting
worldly ends,
all dedicated to
closeness
and the bettering
of my mind
with that which,
but by being so retired,
o'er prized all popular
rate, in
my false brother awaked
an evil nature,
and my trust
like a good parent,
did beget of him a
falsehood in its
contrary
as great as my trust
was, which had
indeed no limit,
a confidence sans bound.
he being thus lorded not
only with what my
revenue yielded
but what my power might
else exact, like one

who,
having into truth by
telling of it, made such
a sinner of his memory
to credit his own lie,
he did believe
he was indeed the duke,
out o'th' substitution
and executing th'
outward face of
royalty with all
prerogative. Hence his
ambition growing-
dost thou hear?

MIRANDA

Your tale sir, would
cure deafness

PROSPERO

To have no screen
between this part he
play'd and him he play'd
it for, he needs will be
absolute Milan. Me, poor
man, my library
was dukedom large
enough:
of temporal royalties
he thinks me now
incapable; confederates-
so dry he was for sway-
wi' the King of Naples
to give him annual
tribute,
do him homage,
subject his coronet to
his crown and bend the
dukedom yet unbow'd--
alas, poor Milan!--
to most ignoble
stooping.

MIRANDA

O the heavens!

PROSPERO

Mark his condition and
the event; then tell me

if this might be a
brother.

MIRANDA

I should sin to think
but nobly of my
grandmother:
good wombs have borne
bad sons.

PROSPERO

Now the condition.
The King of Naples,
being an enemy to me
inveterate, hearkens my
brother's suit;
which was, that he,
in lieu o' the premises
of homage and I know not
how much tribute,
should presently
extirpate me and mine
out of the dukedom
and confer fair Milan
with all the honours
on my brother: whereon,
a treacherous army
levied,
one midnight fated to
the purpose did Antonio
open the gates of Milan,
and, i' the dead of
darkness,
the ministers for the
purpose hurried thence
me and thy crying self.

MIRANDA

Alack, for pity!
I, not remembering
how I cried out then,
will cry it o'er again:
it is a hint
that wrings mine eyes
to't.

PROSPERO

Hear a little further
and then I'll bring thee

to the present business
which now's upon's;
without the which
this story
were most impertinent.

MIRANDA

Wherefore did they not
that hour destroy us?

PROSPERO

Well demanded, wench:
my tale provokes that
question. Dear, they
durst not,
so dear the love my
people bore me, nor set
a mark so bloody
on the business,
but with colours fairer
painted their foul ends.
In few, they hurried us
aboard a bark,
bore us some leagues to
sea;
where they prepared
a rotten carcass of a
boat,
not rigg'd, nor tackle,
sail,
nor mast;
the very rats
instinctively had quit
it: there they hoist us,
to cry to the sea that
roar'd to us, to sigh to
the winds
whose pity, sighing back
again,
did us but loving wrong.

MIRANDA

Alack,
what trouble was I then
to you!

PROSPERO

O, a cherubim thou wast
that did preserve me.

Thou didst smile.
Infused with a fortitude
from heaven,
when I have deck'd the
sea
with drops full salt,
under my burthen
groan'd;
which raised in me
an undergoing stomach,
to bear up against what
should ensue.

MIRANDA

How came we ashore?

PROSPERO

By providence divine.
Some food we had
and some fresh water
that a noble Neapolitan,
Gonzalo,
out of his charity,
being then appointed
master of this design,
did give us, with rich
garments, linens, stuffs
and necessaries,
which since have steaded
much;
so, of his gentleness,
knowing I loved my
books,
he furnish'd me
from mine own library
with volumes that prize
above my dukedom.

MIRANDA

Would I might
but ever see that man!

PROSPERO

Now I arise:

Resumes his mantle

Sit still, and hear

the last of our sea-
sorrow.
Here in this island we
arrived;
and here have I, thy
schoolmaster, made thee
more profit
than other princesses
can
that have more time
for vainer hours and
tutors
not so careful.

                MIRANDA

Heavens thank you for't!
And now, I pray you,
sir,
for still 'tis beating
in my mind, your reason
for raising this sea-
storm?

                PROSPERO

Know thus far forth.
By accident most
strange,
bountiful fortune,
now my dear lady,
hath mine enemies I
brought
to this shore;
and by my prescience
I find my zenith doth
depend upon
a most auspicious star,
whose influence
if now I court not but
omit,
my fortunes will ever
after droop. Here cease
more questions:

Makes hypnotic passes over Miranda

thou art inclined to
sleep;
'tis a good dullness,
and give it way:
I know thou canst not

choose.

Miranda sleeps

Come away, servant,
come.
I am ready now.
Approach, my Ariel,
come.

ENTER Ariel [androgynous/hermaphroditic; with hi-
tech partial dematerialising]

ARIEL

All hail, great master!
Grave sir, hail! I come
to answer thy best
pleasure;
be't to fly, to swim,
to dive into the fire,
to ride on the curl'd
clouds,
to thy strong bidding
task
Ariel and all his
quality.

PROSPERO

Hast thou, spirit,
perform'd
to point the tempest
that I bade thee?

ARIEL

To every article.
I boarded the king's
ship;
now on the beak,
now in the waist, the
deck,
in every cabin, I flamed
amazement: sometime I'd
divide,
and burn in many places;
on the topmast,
the yards and bowsprit,
would I flame
distinctly,
then meet and join.
Jove's lightnings,

the precursors o' the
dreadful thunder-claps,
more momentary
and sight-outrunning
were not;
the fire and cracks
of sulphurous roaring
the most mighty Neptune
seem to besiege
and make his bold waves
tremble,
yea, his dread trident
shake.

PROSPERO

My brave spirit!
Who was so firm,
so constant,
that this coil
would not infect his
reason?

ARIEL

Not a soul but felt
a fever
of the mad and play'd
some tricks of
desperation.
All but mariners
plunged in the foaming
brine
and quit the vessel,
then all afire with me:
the king's son,
Ferdinand,
with hair up-staring,--
then like reeds, not
hair,--
was the first man that
leap'd;
cried, 'hell is empty
and all the devils are
here.'

PROSPERO

Why that's my spirit!
But was not this nigh
shore?

ARIEL

Close by, my master.

PROSPERO

But are they, Ariel,
safe?

ARIEL

Not a hair perish'd;
on their sustaining
garments
not a blemish, but
fresher than before:
and, as thou badest me,
in troops I have
dispersed them
'bout the isle.
The king's son
have I landed
by himself; whom I left
cooling of the air
with sighs
in an odd angle
of the isle
and sitting,
his arms in this sad
knot.

Mimes the miserable Ferdinand

PROSPERO

Of the king's ship
the mariners
say how thou hast
disposed
and all the rest o' the
fleet?

ARIEL

Safely in harbour
is the king's ship;
in the deep nook,
where once thou call'dst
me up
at midnight to fetch dew
from the still-vex'd
bermoothes, there she's
hid: the mariners all
under hatches stow'd;

who,
with a charm join'd to
their suffer'd labour,
I have left asleep;
and for the rest o' the
fleet
which I dispersed,
they all have met again
and are upon the
mediterranean flote,
bound sadly home for
Naples,
supposing that they saw
the king's ship wreck'd
and his great person
perish.

                                    FADES

A place on the island without dwellings. DAY. The
track is rough and gorse abounds. Sitting beneath
a gorse bush by the track, wearing carranes and
sabots under a long homespun dress is a gaunt,
wild looking woman. She is surrounded by tailless
Manx cats. She knits ginger Loghtan wool with
large wooden knitting needles. She pays no
attention to Radcliffe and Shakespeare, but
cackles and repetitively chants:

          Cha daink lesh y gheay
          nagh ragh lesh yn ushtey
          SCREEN SUBTITLES:
          Nothing came with the wind
          that wouldn't go with the
          water

                    RADCLIFFE

This is Joni Joughin.
She is touched but is
without harm.

(To Joni)
Myr y Meoir eu ta mee
cur raaue diu. Gow-shin
arrane dy daaney agh ny
cur-shiu yn fockle er y
fa nagh jig mie ass diu

To Shakespeare after translating

As your Steward I
admonish you. Sing your
heart out but charm not
as no good can come of
it for you.

The people here carry a
great fear of
witchcraft, from Patrick
our patron saint, whose
prayer against
witchcraft is known to
all.
In the time of my late
father's stewardship a
woman of Ronague was
taken without authority
of the Deemster's Assize
at Castletown or the
Lord Bishop's Court at
Kirk Michael. She was
forced into a herring
barrel and rolled a
thousand feet down Cronk
ny Arrey Laa into the
sea to drown, if not
already battered to
death.

(To Joni)
Crytt-shiu laueanyh dou
Yoni.
Nagh abbyr-shiu yn
fockle.
Yioym thoo noa son nys
gott faarnagh.

RADCLIFFE translates to Shakespeare
Knit me gloves Joni.
Cease charms.
I will get new thatch
for your leaking
cottage.

Radcliffe and Shakespeare move on EXEUNT

FADES

PROSPERO

Ariel,
thy charge exactly is

perform'd: but there's
more work.
What is the time o' the
day?

ARIEL

Past the mid season.

PROSPERO

At least two glasses.
The time 'twixt six and
now
must by us both be spent
most preciously.

ARIEL

Is there more toil?
Since thou dost give me
pains,
let me remember thee
what thou hast promised,
which is not yet
perform'd me.

PROSPERO

How now? Moody?
What is't thou canst
demand?

ARIEL

My liberty.

PROSPERO

Before the time be out?
No more!

ARIEL

I prithee, remember
I have done thee worthy
service;
told thee no lies,
made thee no mistakings,
served without or grudge
or grumblings:
thou didst promise
to bate me a full year.

                    PROSPERO

          Dost thou forget
          from what a torment
          I did free thee?

                    ARIEL

          No.

                    PROSPERO

          Thou dost, and think'st
          it much to tread the
          ooze of the salt deep,
          to run upon the sharp
          wind
          of the north,
          to do me business
          in the veins o' the
          earth
          when it is baked with
          frost.

                    ARIEL

          I do not, sir.

                    PROSPERO

          Thou liest, malignant
          thing!
          Hast thou forgot the
          foul witch Sycorax, who
          with age and envy
          was grown into a hoop?
          Hast thou forgot her?

[INSET: {Joni Joughin} **Sycorax** in manic poses]

                    ARIEL

          No, sir.

                    PROSPERO

          Thou hast. Where was she
          born? Speak; tell me.

                    ARIEL

          Sir,in Argier.

PROSPERO

O, was she so?
I must once in a month
recount
what thou hast been,
which thou forget'st.
This damn'd witch
Sycorax,
for mischiefs manifold
and sorceries terrible
to enter human hearing,
from Argier,
thou know'st,
was banish'd:
for one thing she did
they would not take her
life.
Is not this true?

ARIEL

Ay, sir.

FADES

DAY. Manx countryside. A man is working four-
horned Loghtan sheep in a small drystone-walled
field. There are geese grazing in the next small
field. The man is huge and misshapen.

RADCLIFFE to Shakespeare

I have Derby's business
with this man Callinan,
as I will explain you.
His nickname -such as is
common here- is Danny
the Moo.

RADCLIFFE to Danny

*Laa mie Ghannee. Kys ta
shiu jiu?*

*How now Danny. How fare
you today?*

DANNY

*Olk dy hior, olk dy
hior. T'ad taghyssagh,
t'ad taghyssagh. Ta mee*

                    screeby, ta mee screeby,
                    agh cha nel ny meeyllyn
                    as ny jiarganyn rieau
                    faagail. T'ad greimmey
                    as t'ad greimmey as ta
                    mish soutaghey myr booa.
                    Moo oh Moo.

RADCLIFFE translates to Shakespeare
                    Middlin bad, middlin
                    bad. They itch, they
                    itch. I scratch, I
                    scratch, but the lice
                    and the fleas they never
                    leave. They bite and
                    they bite and I moan
                    like a cow Moo oh Moo

Danny enacts all these effects

                         RADCLIFFE to Danny

                    Ayns traa yn Nollick she
                    daa yuiy yeig yn
                    chirveish eu da'n Charn
                    Stanlagh

RAQDCLIFFE translates to Shakespeare
                    At Christmastide your
                    service to Lord Stanley
                    is a dozen geese.

                         DANNY

                    Myr ta shiu fakin cha
                    nel aym agh jeigh. Ga
                    nagh vel lettryn aym agh
                    m'ennym, she coonteyder
                    mie

RADCLIFFE translates to Shakespeare
                    As you see I have but
                    ten. Although I have no
                    letters but my name, I
                    am a good counter

                         RADCLIFFE to Danny

                    S'liooar jeigh. Cha nel
                    Chiarn jooigh agh shegin
                    da cur bee da mooarane
                    sleih

RADCLIFFE translates to Shakespeare
Ten will suffice. His
lordship is not greedy
but has many mouths to
feed.

DANNY

*Foddee dy vreillym nane
son y voayrd Nollick aym
pene.*

RADCLIFFE translates to Shakespeare
I may keep one for my
own Christmas table.

RADCLIFFE to Danny

*Nuy myr shen Ghannee.
Verrym lhiam ad lesh my
chairt marish y chooid
Nollick elley.*

RADCLIFFE translates to Shakespeare
Nine it is Danny.
I will fetch them with
my cart with the other
Christmas dues.

DANNY

*Nuy myr shen Veoir
Radlagh*

RADCLIFFE translates to Shakespeare
*Nine it is Steward
Radcliffe*

RADCLIFFE to Shakespeare

Callinan is, or saith he
is, infested with fleas
and lice. He also is
touched, but without
harm. His service to
Stanley is a dozen geese
at Christmas. We settled
for nine this year.

Radcliffe and Shakespeare depart from Danny who

moans and itches again

EXEUNT

                                        FADES

                    PROSPERO

[Sycorax again INSET with prodigious pregnancy]

                This blue-eyed hag was
                hither brought
                with child
                and here was left by the
                sailors. Thou, my slave,
                as thou report'st
                thyself,
                wast then her servant;
                and,for thou wast a
                spirit
                too delicate
                to act her earthy and
                abhorr'd commands,
                refusing her grand
                hests, she did confine
                thee, by help of her
                more potent ministers
                and in her most
                unmitigable rage,
                into a cloven pine;
                within which rift
                imprison'd
                thou didst painfully
                remain
                a dozen years;
                within which space she
                died
                and left thee there;
                where thou didst vent
                thy groans
                as fast as mill-wheels
                strike.
                Then was this island--
                save for the son
                that she did litter
                here,
                a freckled whelp hag-
                born--
                not honour'd with a
                human shape.

[End Sycorax inset]

ARIEL

Yes, Caliban her son.

PROSPERO

Dull thing, I say so;
he,
that Caliban whom now
I keep in service.
Thou best know'st
what torment I did find
thee in;
thy groans did make
wolves howl
and penetrate the
breasts
of ever angry bears:
it was a torment
to lay upon the damn'd,
which Sycorax could not
again undo: it was mine
art,
when I arrived and heard
thee,
that made gape the pine
and let thee out.

ARIEL

I thank thee, master.

PROSPERO

If thou more murmur'st,
I will rend an oak
and peg thee in his
knotty entrails till
thou hast howl'd away
twelve winters.

ARIEL

Pardon, master;
I will be correspondent
to command
and do my spiriting
gently.

PROSPERO

Do so, and after two
days

I will discharge thee.

ARIEL

That's my noble master!
What shall I do? Say
what;
what shall I do?

PROSPERO

Go make thyself
like a nymph o' the sea:
be subject to no sigh
but thine and mine,
invisible to every
eyeball else.
Go take this shape
and hither come in't:
go, hence with
diligence!

EXIT Ariel

Awake, dear heart,
awake!
Thou hast slept well;
awake!

MIRANDA

The strangeness of your
story
put heaviness in me.

PROSPERO

Shake it off. Come on;
We'll visit Caliban my
slave,
who never yields us kind
answer.

MIRANDA

'tis a villain, sir,
I do not love to look
on.

PROSPERO

But, as 'tis, we cannot
miss him: he does make

our fire,
fetch in our wood
and serves in offices
that profit us.
What, ho! Slave!
Caliban!
Thou earth, thou! Speak.

CALIBAN (O.S)

There's wood enough

PROSPERO

Come forth, I say!
There's other business
for thee:
come, thou tortoise!
When?

RE-ENTER Ariel like a water-nymph

Fine apparition!
My quaint Ariel,
hark in thine ear.

ARIEL

My lord it shall be
done.

EXIT

PROSPERO

Thou poisonous slave,
got by the devil himself
upon thy wicked dam,
come forth!

ENTER {Callinan}Caliban

CALIBAN

As wicked dew
as e'er my mother
brush'd
with raven's feather
from unwholesome fen
drop on you both!
A south-west blow on ye
and blister you all
o'er!

PROSPERO

For this, be sure,
to-night thou shalt have
cramps,
side-stitches
that shall pen thy
breath up;
urchins shall,
for that vast of night
that they may work, all
exercise on thee; thou
shalt be pinch'd
as thick as honeycomb,
each pinch more stinging
than bees that made 'em.

CALIBAN

I must eat my dinner.
This island's mine,
by Sycorax my mother,
which thou takest
from me.
When thou camest first,
thou strokedst me and
madest much of me,
wouldst give me
water with berries in't,
and teach me how to name
the bigger light, and
how the less,
that burn by day and
night:
and then I loved thee
and show'd thee all the
qualities o' the isle,
the fresh springs,
brine-pits, barren place
and fertile:
cursed be I that did so!
All the charms of
Sycorax,
toads, beetles, bats,
light on you!
For I
am all the subjects that
you have,
which first was mine own
king:
and here you sty me
in this hard rock,

whiles you do keep from
me
the rest o' the island.

PROSPERO

Thou most lying slave,
whom stripes may move,
not kindness!
I have used thee,
filth as thou art, with
human care, and lodged
thee in mine own cell,
till thou didst seek to
violate
the honour of my child.

CALIBAN

O ho, O ho! Would't had
been done!
Thou didst prevent me;
I had peopled else
this isle with Calibans.

PROSPERO

Abhorred slave,
which any print of
goodness wilt not take,
being capable of all
ill! I pitied thee,
took pains to make thee
speak, taught thee each
hour one thing or other:
when thou didst not,
savage,
know thine own meaning,
but wouldst gabble
like a thing most
brutish,
I endow'd thy purposes
with words that made
them known.
But thy vile race,
though thou didst learn,
had that in't which good
natures
could not abide to be
with; therefore wast
thou deservedly confined
into this rock, who

hadst deserved more than
a prison.

CALIBAN

You taught me language;
and my profit on't is,
I know how to curse.
The red plague rid you
for learning me your
language!

PROSPERO

Hag-seed, hence!
Fetch us in fuel;
and be quick, thou'rt
best,
to answer other
business.
Shrug'st thou, malice?
If thou neglect'st
or dost unwillingly
what I command,
I'll rack thee with old
cramps,
fill all thy bones
with aches,
make thee roar that
beasts shall tremble
at thy din.

CALIBAN

No, pray thee.

(Aside)
I must obey:
his art is of such
power,
it would control my
dam's god, Setebos,
and make a vassal of
him.

PROSPERO

So, slave; hence!

EXIT Caliban

RE-ENTER Ariel, invisible, playing and singing;
{Radcliffe} Ferdinand following

Ariel's song.
[Fasletto/Counter-tenor]

ARIEL

Come unto these yellow
sands,
and then take hands:
courtsied when you have
and kiss'd
the wild waves whist,
foot it featly here and
there;
and, sweet sprites,
the burthen bear.
Hark, hark!

    (Burthen
     dispersedly,
     within)
The watch-dogs bark!
Burthen: Bow-wow [hounds
belling]
Hark, hark! I hear the
strain
of strutting chanticleer
cry, cock-a-diddle-dow.
[cock's crow]

FERDINAND

Where should this music
be?
I' the air or the earth?
It sounds no more: and
sure,
it waits upon
some god o' the island.
Sitting on a bank,
weeping again
the king my father's
wreck,
this music crept by me
upon the waters,
allaying both their fury
and my passion with its
sweet air: thence I have
follow'd it,
or it hath drawn me
rather.
But 'tis gone.
No, it begins again.

ARIEL sings

Full fathom five thy
father lies;
of his bones are coral
made;
those are pearls
that were his eyes:
nothing of him that doth
fade
but doth suffer a sea-
change
into something rich and
strange.
Sea-nymphs hourly ring
his knell

     (Burthen: Ding-
        dong [bells
        chime])

Hark! Now I hear them,--
ding-dong, bell. [bells
chime]

          FERDINAND

The ditty does remember
my drown'd father.
This is no mortal
business,
nor no sound that the
earth owes.
I hear it now above me.

          PROSPERO: [to Miranda]

The fringed curtains of
thine eye advance
and say
what thou seest yond.

          MIRANDA

What is't? A spirit?
Lord,
how it looks about!
Believe me, sir,
it carries a brave form.
But 'tis a spirit.

          PROSPERO

No, wench;
it eats and sleeps
and hath such senses
as we have, such.
This gallant
which thou seest
was in the wreck; and,
but he's something
stain'd
with grief that's
beauty's canker, thou
mightst call him a
goodly person: he hath
lost his fellows
and strays about
to find 'em.

MIRANDA

I might call him a thing
divine, for nothing
natural
I ever saw so noble.

PROSPERO [Aside]

It goes on, I see as my
soul prompts it

[To Ariel]

Spirit, fine spirit I'll
free thee within two
days for this

FERDINAND

Most sure, the goddess
on whom these airs
attend!
Vouchsafe my prayer may
know
if you remain upon this
island;
and that you will some
good instruction give
how I may bear me here:
my prime request,
which I do last
pronounce, is,
O you wonder!

If you be maid or no?

MIRANDA

No wonder, sir;
but certainly a maid.

FERDINAND

My language! Heavens!
I am the best of them
that speak this speech,
were I but where 'tis
spoken.

PROSPERO

How? The best?
What wert thou, if the
king of Naples heard
thee?

FERDINAND

A single thing,
as I am now,
that wonders to hear
thee speak of Naples.
He does hear me;
and that he does I weep:
myself am Naples,
who with mine eyes,
never since at ebb,
beheld the king
my father wreck'd.

MIRANDA

Alack, for mercy!

FERDINAND

Yes, faith, and all his
lords;
the Duke of Milan
and his brave son being
twain.

PROSPERO [Aside]

The Duke of Milan
and his more braver
daughter could

control thee
if you were
fit to do't.
At the first sight they
have changed eyes

(To ARIEL}

Delicate Ariel I'll set
you free for this

   (To FERDINAND}

A word, good sir;
I fear you have done
yourself some wrong:
a word.

          MIRANDA

Why speaks my father so
ungently? This is the
third man
that e'er I saw,
The first that e'er I
sigh'd for: pity move my
father
to be inclined my way!

          FERDINAND

O, if a virgin,
and your affection not
gone forth, I'll make
you
the queen of Naples.

          PROSPERO

Soft, sir! One word
more.

    (Aside)
They are both in
either's powers; but
this swift business
I must uneasy make,
lest too light winning
make the prize light.

(To FERDINAND)

One word more;
I charge thee
that thou attend me:
thou dost here usurp
the name thou ownest
not;
and hast put thyself
upon this island
as a spy,
to win it from me,
the lord on't.

FERDINAND

No, as I am a man.

MIRANDA

There's nothing ill
can dwell
in such a temple:
if the ill spirit
have so fair a house,
good things
will strive to dwell
with't.

PROSPERO

Follow me.
Speak not you for him;
he's a traitor. Come;
I'll manacle thy neck
and feet together:
sea-water shalt thou
drink;
thy food shall be
the fresh-brook muscles,
wither'd roots and husks
wherein the acorn
cradled. Follow.

FERDINAND

No;
I will resist such
entertainment till mine
enemy has more power.

Draws, and is charmed from moving

MIRANDA

O dear father,
make not too rash a
trial of him, for he's
gentle and not fearful.

PROSPERO

What? I say, my foot my
tutor?
Put thy sword up,
traitor;
who makest a show
but darest not strike,
thy conscience is so
possess'd with guilt:
come from thy ward,
for I can here disarm
thee with this stick
and make thy weapon
drop.

MIRANDA

Beseech you, father.

[Miranda grabs Prospero's sleeve]

PROSPERO

Hence! Hang not on my
garments.

MIRANDA

Sir, have pity;
I'll be his surety.

PROSPERO

Silence! One word more
shall make me chide
thee,
if not hate thee. What!
An advocate for an
imposter! Hush!
Thou think'st there is
no more such shapes as
he,
having seen but him and
Caliban: foolish wench!
To the most of men this
is a Caliban

and they to him are
angels.

                MIRANDA

My affections
are then most humble;
I have no ambition
to see a goodlier man.

                PROSPERO

[Again making hypnotic passes]

Come on; obey:
thy nerves are in their
infancy again and have
no vigour in them.

                FERDINAND

So they are; my spirits,
as in a dream,
are all bound up.
My father's loss,
the weakness which I
feel,
the wreck of all my
friends,
nor this man's threats,
to whom I am subdued,
are but light to me,
might I but through my
prison
once a day behold this
maid:
all corners else o' the
earth
let liberty make use of;
space enough
have I in such a prison.

                PROSPERO
[Aside]

It works. Come on.
Thou hast done well,
fine Ariel!

[To Ferdinand]

Follow me.

[To Ariel]

Hark what thou else
shalt do me.

MIRANDA

Be of comfort;
my father's of a better
nature, sir, than he
appears by speech: this
is unwonted
which now came from him.

PROSPERO

Thou shalt be free
as mountain winds:
but then exactly do
all points of my
command.

ARIEL

To the syllable.

PROSPERO

Come, follow. Speak not
for him.

EXEUNT

Another part of the island.

ENTER ALONSO, SEBASTIAN, ANTONIO, GONZALO,
ADRIAN, FRANCISCO, and others

GONZALO

Beseech you, sir, be
merry;
you have cause,
so have we all, of joy;
for our escape
is much beyond our loss.
Our hint of woe is
common;
every day some sailor's
wife,
the masters of some
merchant
and the merchant

have just our theme of
woe;
but for the miracle,
I mean our preservation,
few in millions can
speak like us: then
wisely, good sir,
weigh our sorrow with
our comfort.

                    SEBASTIAN [to Antonio]

He receives comfort
like cold porridge.

                    ANTONIO [to Sebastian]

The visitor will not
give him o'er so.

                    SEBASTIAN

Look he's winding up the
watch of his wit; by and
by it will strike.

                    GONZALO [to Alonso]

Sir,--

                    SEBASTIAN

One: tell.

                    GONZALO

When every grief
is entertain'd that's
offer'd,
Comes to the
entertainer--
therefore, my lord,--

                    ANTONIO

Fie, what a spendthrift
is he
of his tongue!

                    GONZALO

Well, I have done: but

yet,--

SEBASTIAN

He will be talking.

ADRIAN

Though this island seem
to be desert,--
uninhabitable
and almost
inaccessible,--

ANTONIO

He could not miss't.

ADRIAN

It must needs be of
subtle,
tender and delicate
temperance.
The air breathes upon us
here
most sweetly.

GONZALO

Here is everything
advantageous to life.

ANTONIO

True; save means to
live.

SEBASTIAN

Of that there's none, or
little.

GONZALO

How lush and lusty the
grass looks! How green!
But the rarity of it
is,-- which
is indeed almost beyond
credit,
-- that our garments,

being,
as they were, drenched
in the sea,
hold notwithstanding
their freshness and
glosses,
being rather new-dyed
than stained with salt
water.
Methinks our garments
are now
as fresh as when we put
them on first in Afric,
at the marriage of
the king's fair daughter
Claribel to the King of
Tunis.

SEBASTIAN

'Twas a sweet marriage,
and we prosper well in
our return.

ADRIAN

Tunis was never graced
before with such a
paragon to their queen.

GONZALO

Not since widow Dido's
time.
Sir, we were talking
that our garments seem
now as fresh as
when we were at Tunis
at the marriage
of your daughter,
who is now queen.

ANTONIO

And the rarest that e'er
came there.

GONZALO

Is not, sir, my doublet
as fresh as the first
day I wore it?
I mean, in a sort when I

wore it at your
daughter's marriage?

ALONSO

You cram these words
into mine ears
against the stomach of
my sense. Would I had
never married
my daughter there!
For, coming thence,
My son is lost and,
in my rate, she too,
who is so far from Italy
removed
I ne'er again shall see
her.
O thou mine heir
of Naples and of Milan,
what strange fish
hath made his meal on
thee?

FRANCISCO

Sir, he may live:
I saw him beat the
surges under him, and
ride upon their backs;
he trod the water,
whose enmity he flung
aside,
and breasted the surge
most swoln that met him;
his bold head
'bove the contentious
waves
he kept, and oar'd
himself
with his good arms in
lusty stroke to the
shore, that o'er his
wave-worn basis bow'd,
as stooping to relieve
him:
I not doubt he came
alive to land.

ALONSO

No, no, he's gone.

SEBASTIAN

Sir, you may thank
yourself
for this great loss,
that would not bless our
Europe with your
daughter,
but rather lose her to
an African;
where she at least
is banish'd from your
eye, who hath cause to
wet the grief on't.
You were kneel'd to and
importuned otherwise by
all of us,
and the fair soul
herself, weigh'd between
loathness and obedience,
at which end o' the beam
should bow. We have lost
your son,
I fear, for ever:
Milan and Naples have
more widows in them of
this business' making
than we bring men to
comfort them:
the fault's your own.

GONZALO

My lord Sebastian,
the truth you speak
doth lack some
gentleness
and time to speak it in:
you rub the sore,
when you should bring
the plaster.
It is foul weather in us
all,
good sir, when you are
cloudy.

ANTONIO

Very foul.

GONZALO

Had I plantation of this
isle, my lord,--

ANTONIO

He'ld sow't with nettle-
seed.

SEBASTIAN

Or docks, or mallows.

GONZALO

And were the king on't,
what would I do?

SEBASTIAN

'Scape being drunk for
want of wine.

GONZALO

I' the commonwealth
I would by contraries
execute all things;
for no kind of traffic
would I admit;
no name of magistrate;
letters should not be
known;
riches, poverty,
And use of service,
none;
contract, succession,
bourn, bound of land,
tilth, vineyard, none;
no use of metal, corn,
or wine,
or oil;
no occupation; all men
idle, all;
and women too,
but innocent and pure;
no sovereignty;--

SEBASTIAN

Yet he would be king

on't.

ANTONIO

The latter end of his
commonwealth forgets the
beginning.

GONZALO

All things in common
nature should produce
without sweat or
endeavour: treason,
felony, Sword, pike,
knife, gun, or need of
any engine,
would I not have;
but nature should bring
forth,
of its own kind, all
foison,
all abundance, to feed
my innocent people.

SEBASTIAN

No marrying 'mong his
subjects?

ANTONIO

None, man; all idle:
whores and knaves.

GONZALO

I would with such
perfection govern, sir,
to excel the golden age.
and,-- do you mark me,
sir?
I do well believe your
highness; and did it to
minister occasion
to these gentlemen,
who are of such sensible
and nimble lungs that
they always use to laugh
at nothing.

ANTONIO

'Twas you we laughed at.

GONZALO

Who in this kind
of merry fooling
am nothing to you:
so you may continue and
laugh at nothing still.

ANTONIO

What a blow was there
given!

GONZALO

You are gentlemen of
brave metal; you would
lift the moon
out of her sphere,
if she would continue
in it five weeks
without changing.

ENTER ARIEL, invisible, playing solemn music

SEBASTIAN

We would so,
and then go a bat-
fowling.

ANTONIO

Nay, good my lord, be
not angry.

GONZALO

No, I warrant you;
I will not adventure
my discretion so weakly.
Will you laugh me
asleep,
for I am very heavy?

ANTONIO

Go sleep, and hear us.

All sleep except ALONSO, SEBASTIAN, and ANTONIO

                    ALONSO

          What,
          all so soon asleep!
          I wish mine eyes
          Would, with themselves,
          shut up my thoughts:
          I find
          they are inclined
          to do so.

                    SEBASTIAN

          Please you, sir,
          Do not omit the heavy
          offer of it:
          It seldom visits sorrow;
          when it doth, it is a
          comforter.

                    ANTONIO

          We two, my lord,
          will guard your person
          while you take your
          rest,
          and watch your safety.

                    ALONSO

          Thank you. Wondrous
          heavy.

ALONSO sleeps. EXIT ARIEL

                    SEBASTIAN

          What a strange
          drowsiness
          possesses them!

                    ANTONIO

          It is the quality o' the
          climate.

                    SEBASTIAN

          Why doth it not then

our eyelids sink?
I find not myself
disposed to sleep.

ANTONIO

Nor I;
my spirits are nimble.
They fell together all,
as by consent;
they dropp'd,
as by a thunder-stroke.
What might,
worthy Sebastian?
O, what might?--no
more:--
and yet me thinks
I see it in thy face,
what thou shouldst be:
the occasion speaks
thee,
and my strong
imagination
sees a crown
dropping upon thy head.

SEBASTIAN

What, art thou waking?

ANTONIO

Do you not hear me
speak?

SEBASTIAN

I do;
and surely it is a
sleepy language and thou
speak'st
out of thy sleep.
What is it thou didst
say?
This is a strange
repose,
to be asleep with eyes
wide open; standing,
speaking, moving,
And yet so fast asleep.

ANTONIO

Noble Sebastian,
thou let'st thy fortune
sleep--
die, rather; wink'st
whiles thou art waking.

SEBASTIAN

Thou dost snore
distinctly;
there's meaning in thy
snores.

ANTONIO

I am more serious than
my custom: you must be
so too, if heed me;
which to do
trebles thee o'er. O,
If you but knew how you
the purpose cherish
whiles thus you mock it!

SEBASTIAN

Prithee, say on:
the setting of thine eye
and cheek proclaim a
matter from thee,
and a birth indeed
which throes thee much
to yield.

ANTONIO

Thus, sir:
although this lord of
weak remembrance, this,
who shall be of as
little memory
when he is earth'd,
o' hath here almost
persuade,--
for he's a spirit of
persuasion, only
professes to persuade,--
the king his son's
alive,
'tis as impossible that
he's undrown'd and he

that sleeps here swims.

                SEBASTIAN

I have no hope
that he's undrown'd.

                ANTONIO

O, out of that 'no hope'
what great hope
have you!
No hope that way is
another way so high
a hope
that even ambition
cannot pierce a wink
beyond,
but doubt discovery
there.
Will you grant with me
that Ferdinand is
drown'd?

                SEBASTIAN

He's gone.

                ANTONIO

Then, tell me, who's
the next heir of Naples?

                SEBASTIAN

Claribel.

                ANTONIO

She that is
Queen of Tunis;
she that dwells
ten leagues beyond man's
life;
she that from Naples
can have no note,
unless the sun were
post--
the man i' the moon's
too slow--till new-born
chins
be rough and razorable;
she that--from whom?

We all were sea-
swallow'd,
though some cast again,
and by that destiny
to perform an act
whereof what's past is
prologue, what to come
in yours and my
discharge.

SEBASTIAN

What stuff is this!
How say you? 'tis true,
my brother's daughter's
Queen of Tunis;
so is she heir of
Naples;
'twixt which regions
There is some space.

ANTONIO

A space
whose every cubit
seems to cry out,
'How shall that Claribel
measure us back
to Naples?
Keep in Tunis,
and let Sebastian wake.
Say, this were death
that now hath seized
them; why, they were no
worse
than now they are.
There be that can rule
Naples
as well as he that
sleeps;
lords that can prate
as amply and
unnecessarily
as this Gonzalo;
I myself could make
a chough
of as deep chat.
O, that you bore
the mind that I do!
what a sleep were this
for your advancement!
Do you understand me?

SEBASTIAN

Methinks I do.

ANTONIO

And how does your
content
tender your own good
fortune?

SEBASTIAN

I remember you did
supplant
your brother Prospero.

ANTONIO

True:
and look how well
my garments sit upon me;
much feater than before:
my brother's servants
were then my fellows;
now they are my men.

SEBASTIAN

But, for your
conscience?

ANTONIO

Ay, sir;
where lies that?
if 'twere a kibe,
'twould put me to my
slipper:
but I feel not
this deity in my bosom:
twenty consciences,
that stand 'twixt me and
Milan, candied be they
and melt ere they
molest!
Here lies your brother,
no better than the earth
he lies upon,
if he were that which
now he's like,
that's dead;

whom I, with this
obedient steel,
three inches of it,
can lay to bed for ever;
whiles you, doing thus,
to the perpetual wink
for aye
might put this ancient
morsel,
this Sir Prudence,
who should not upbraid
our course.
For all the rest,
they'll take suggestion
as a cat laps milk;
they'll tell the clock
to any business that
we say befits the hour.

SEBASTIAN

Thy case, dear friend,
shall be my precedent;
as thou got'st Milan,
I'll come by Naples.
Draw thy sword:
one stroke
shall free thee from the
tribute which thou
payest;
and I the king shall
love thee.

ANTONIO

Draw together;
and when I rear my hand,
do you the like,
to fall it on Gonzalo.

SEBASTIAN

O, but one word.

They talk apart

RE-ENTER ARIEL, invisible

ARIEL

My master
through his art
foresees the danger

that you, his friend,
are in;
and sends me forth--
for else his project
dies--
to keep them living.

Sings in GONZALO's ear

While you here do
snoring lie,
open-eyed conspiracy
His time doth take.
If of life you keep a
care,
shake off slumber, and
beware:
awake, awake!

ANTONIO

Then let us both be sudden. [Draws sword]

GONZALO [wakes]

Now, good angels
preserve the king.

ALONSO [wakes]

Why, how now? ho, awake!
Why are you drawn?
Wherefore this ghastly
looking?

GONZALO

's the matter?

SEBASTIAN

Whiles we stood here
securing your repose,
even now, we heard a
hollow burst of
bellowing like bulls,
or rather lions:
did't not wake you?
It struck mine ear most
terribly.

ALONSO

I heard nothing.

ANTONIO

O, 'twas a din
to fright a monster's
ear,
To make an earthquake!
sure, it was the roar
of a whole herd of
lions.

ALONSO

Heard you this, Gonzalo?

GONZALO

Upon mine honour, sir,
I heard a humming,
and that a strange one
too,
which did awake me:
I shaked you, sir, and
cried:
as mine eyes open'd,
I saw their weapons
drawn:
there was a noise,
that's verily.
'tis best we stand upon
our guard,
or that we quit this
place;
let's draw our weapons.
[All draw their swords]

ALONSO

Lead off this ground;
and let's make further
search
for my poor son.

GONZALO

Heavens keep him from
these beasts!
For he is, sure, i' the
island.

ALONSO

Lead away.

ARIEL

Prospero my lord
shall know
what I have done:
so, king, go safely on
to seek thy son.

EXEUNT. FADES

On the Island. DAY. Two walkers approach
Radcliffe and Shakespeare. One carries several
rabbits on his belt. The other is accompanied by
a lurcher hound. They swig from a shared flask.

RADCLIFFE

These men are known as
Old Jago and Young Jago-
Old and Young James. I
believe them to be
cousins. They live by
catching and disposing
of rabbits and hares
which are plentiful in
this country. They show
little respect for
boundary walls. They
also have a reputation
for strong drink but
their Still has never
been found

OLD JAGO

*Veoir Radlagh
Bannaghtyn. Vel shiu
feme conneeyn?*
[Steward Radcliffe Greetings.
Hast need of rabbits?]

RADCLIFFE

Cha nee gura mie en Yago
[Not today thank you Jago]

Tame polecats appear out of Young Jago's sleeves
and pockets

SHAKESPEARE

In God's name what are
these marmosets?

RADCLIFFE

Nay sir. On this island
there are no wolves nor
foxes. Neither reptiles,
who, it is said were
cast out by Saint
Patrick on his visit to
the island, a visit and
a cause which I doubt
much. He sent his hermit
monks who rowed here in
their leather boats;
their cells remain. The
polecats which you see
thrive on the rabbits
and hares and they may
be tamed and put to
work, since the common
people afford no guns
and would not be
encouraged by Lord
Stanley.

SHAKESPEARE

Very pleasing cats to so
pole-axe me, and these
have a tale to tell
unlike those we saw with
the knitter, or was't it
with the man with nits?

Radcliffe shakes his head, laughs and shrugs

RADCLIFFE to the two Jagos

*Slane eu Yago as Yago. Shaghyn-shiu thalloo yn
Chiarn Stanlagh as sheghin-shiu ny poagaghyn eu.*

Radcliffe translates to Shakespeare

Farewell Jago and Jago. Avoid Lord Stanley's land
and avoid your flasks.

EXEUNT   FAST FADE

Another part of the island.
ENTER CALIBAN with a burden of wood. A noise of
thunder heard

                    CALIBAN

          All the infections
          that the sun sucks up
          from bogs, fens, flats,
          on Prosper fall
          and make him
          by inch-meal a disease!
          His spirits hear me
          and yet I needs must
          curse.
          but they'll nor pinch,
          fright me with urchin--
          shows,
          pitch me i' the mire,
          nor lead me,
          like a firebrand,
          in the dark
          out of my way,
          unless he bid 'em;
          but for every trifle
          are they set upon me;
          sometime like apes
          that mow and chatter at
          me
          and after bite me,
          then like hedgehogs
          which lie tumbling in my
          barefoot way and mount
          their pricks
          at my footfall;
          sometime am I all wound
          with adders
          who with cloven tongues
          do hiss me into madness.

ENTER {Old Jago} TRINCULO
          Lo, now, lo!
          Here comes a spirit of
          his,
          and to torment me
          for bringing wood in
          slowly.
          I'll fall flat;

[lies down]
          perchance he will not
          mind me.

TRINCULO

Here's neither bush nor
shrub,
to bear off any weather
at all,
and another storm
brewing;
I hear it sing i' the
wind:
yond same black cloud,
yond huge one,
looks like a foul
bombard that would shed
his liquor.
If it should thunder
as it did before,
I know not
where to hide my head:
yond same cloud cannot
choose but fall by
pailfuls.
What have we here?
A man or a fish?
dead or alive?
A fish:
he smells like a fish;

He smells the body and holds his nose
a very ancient and fish-
like smell; a kind of
not of the newest Poor-
John. A strange fish!
Were I in England now,
as once I was,
and had but this fish
painted,
not a holiday fool there
but would give a piece
of silver: there would
this monster
make a man;
any strange beast there
makes a man:
when they will not give
a doit to relieve
a lame beggar,
they will lazy out ten
to see a dead Indian.
Legged like a man
and his fins like arms!
Warm o' my troth!

I do now let loose my
opinion;
hold it no longer:
this is no fish,
but an islander,
that hath lately
suffered
by a thunderbolt.

Thunder

Alas,
the storm is come again!
My best way is
to creep under his
gaberdine;
there is no other
shelter hereabouts:
misery acquaints a man
with strange bed-
fellows.
I will here shroud till
the dregs of the storm
be past.

[Crawls under Caliban, his legs exposed]

ENTER {Young Jago}STEPHANO, singing: a bottle in
his hand

STEPHANO

I shall no more to sea,
to sea,
here shall I die ashore-
this is a very scurvy
tune to sing
at a man's funeral:
well, here's my comfort.

Drinks

Sings:

The master, the swabber,
the boatswain and I,
the gunner and his mate
loved Mall, Meg and
Marian and Margery,
but none of us cared for
Kate;
for she had a tongue
with a tang,
would cry to a sailor,
go hang!
She loved not the savour

of tar nor of pitch,
Yet a tailor might
scratch her where'er she
did itch:
then to sea, boys,
and let her go hang!
This is a scurvy tune
too:
but here's my comfort.

Drinks

CALIBAN

Do not torment me: Oh!

STEPHANO

What's the matter?
Have we devils here?
Do you put
tricks upon's with
savages
and men of Ind, ha?
I have not scaped
drowning
to be afeard now
of your four legs;
for it hath been said,
as proper a man as
ever went on four legs
cannot make him give
ground;
and it shall be said so
again while Stephano
breathes at's nostrils.

CALIBAN

The spirit torments me;
Oh!

STEPHANO

This is some monster of
the isle with four legs,
who hath got,
as I take it, an ague.
Where the devil
should he learn our
language?
I will give him some
relief,

if it be but for that.
If I can recover him
and keep him tame
and get to Naples
with him,
he's a present
for any emperor
that ever trod
on neat's leather.

CALIBAN

Do not torment me,
prithee;
I'll bring my wood home
faster.

STEPHANO

He's in his fit now and
does not talk after the
wisest.
He shall taste of my
bottle:
if he have never drunk
wine afore will go near
to remove his fit.
If I can recover him
and keep him tame,
I will not take too much
for him; he shall pay
for him that hath him,
and that soundly.

CALIBAN

Thou dost me yet but
little hurt; thou wilt
anon,
I know it by thy
trembling:
now Prosper works upon
thee.

STEPHANO

Come on your ways; open
your mouth; here is that
which will give language
to you, cat: open your
mouth;
this will shake your
shaking,

I can tell you, and that
soundly: you cannot tell
who's your friend:
open your chaps again.

Pours drink into Caliban's mouth

TRINCULO

I should know that
voice:
it should be--but he is
drowned;
and these are devils: O
defend me!

STEPHANO

Four legs and two
voices:
a most delicate monster!
His forward voice now
is to speak well of his
friend;
his backward voice
is to utter foul
speeches
and to detract.
If all the wine in my
bottle will
recover him, I will help
his ague. Come. Amen! I
will pour some
in thy other mouth.

Pours drink into Caliban's rear

TRINCULO

Stephano!

STEPHANO

Doth thy other mouth
call me? Mercy, mercy!
This is a devil,
and no monster:
I will leave him;
I have no long spoon.

TRINCULO

Stephano! If thou beest

Stephano, touch me and
speak to me:
for I am Trinculo-
be not afeard-
thy good friend
Trinculo.

STEPHANO

If thou beest Trinculo,
come forth: I'll pull
thee by the lesser legs:
if any be Trinculo's
legs,
these are they.
Thou art very Trinculo
indeed!
How camest thou to be
the siege of this moon-
calf?
Can he vent Trinculos?

Pulls at Trinculo's protruding legs

TRINCULO

I took him to be killed
with a thunder-stroke.
But art thou not
drowned, Stephano?
I hope now thou art
not drowned.
Is the storm overblown?
I hid me under the dead
moon-calf's gaberdine
for fear of the storm.
And art thou living,
Stephano? O
Stephano, two
Neapolitans 'scaped!

STEPHANO

Prithee, do not turn me
about;
my stomach is not
constant.

CALIBAN [ASIDE]

These be fine things,
an' if they be not
sprites.

That's a brave god
and bears celestial
liquor.
I will kneel to him.

                STEPHANO

How didst thou 'scape?
How camest thou hither?
Swear by this bottle
how thou camest hither.
I escaped
upon a butt of sack
which the sailors heaved
o'erboard, by this
bottle; which I made of
the bark of a tree
with mine own hands
since I was cast ashore.

                CALIBAN [kneeling]

I'll swear upon that
bottle
to be thy true subject;
for the liquor is not
earthly.

                STEPHANO

Here;
swear then how thou
escapedst.

                TRINCULO

Swum ashore, man,
like a duck:
I can swim like a duck,
I'll be sworn.

                STEPHANO

Here, kiss the book.
Though thou canst swim
like a duck,
thou art made like a
goose.

                TRINCULO

O Stephano, hast any
more of this?

Holding out empty bottle

                    STEPHANO

          The whole butt, man:
          my cellar is in a rock
          by the sea-side
          where my wine is hid.
          How now, moon-calf!
          How does thine ague?

                    CALIBAN

          Hast thou not dropp'd
          from heaven?

                    STEPHANO
          Out o' the moon, I do
          assure thee: I was the
          man i' the moon
          when time was.

                    CALIBAN

          I have seen thee in her
          and I do adore thee:
          My mistress show'd me
          thee
          and thy dog and thy
          bush.

                    STEPHANO

          Come, swear to that;
          kiss the book:
          I will furnish it anon
          with new contents swear.

                    TRINCULO

          By this good light,
          this is a very shallow
          monster!
          I afeard of him!
          A very weak monster!
          The man i' the moon!
          A most poor credulous
          monster!
          Well drawn, monster,
          in good sooth!

                    CALIBAN

I'll show thee every
fertile inch o' th'
island;
and I will kiss thy
foot:
I prithee, be my god.

TRINCULO

By this light, a most
perfidious and drunken
monster!
when's god's asleep,
he'll rob his bottle.

CALIBAN

I'll kiss thy foot;
I'll swear myself thy
subject.

STEPHANO

Come on then; down, and
swear.

Caliban kisses Stephano's foot

TRINCULO

I shall laugh myself to
death
at this puppy-headed
monster.
A most scurvy monster!
I could find in my heart
to beat him,--

STEPHANO

Come, kiss.

TRINCULO

But that the poor
monster's
in drink: an abominable
monster!

CALIBAN

I'll show thee the best
springs; I'll pluck thee

berries;
I'll fish for thee
and get thee wood
enough.
A plague upon the tyrant
that I serve!
I'll bear him no more
sticks,
but follow thee,
thou wondrous man.

TRINCULO

A most ridiculous
monster,
to make a wonder
of a poor drunkard!

CALIBAN

I prithee,
let me bring thee
where crabs grow;
and I with my long nails
will dig thee pignuts;
show thee a jay's nest
and instruct thee
how to snare the nimble
marmoset; I'll bring
thee
to clustering filberts
and sometimes I'll get
thee
young scallops from the
rock.
Wilt thou go with me?

STEPHANO

I prithee now,
lead the way
without any more
talking.
Trinculo, the king
and all our company else
being drowned,
we will inherit here:
here; bear my bottle:
fellow Trinculo,
we'll fill him by and by
again.

CALIBAN

[Sings drunkenly]

Farewell master;
farewell, farewell!

TRINCULO

A howling monster:
a drunken monster!

CALIBAN

No more dams I'll make
for fish
nor fetch in firing
at requiring;
nor scrape trencher, nor
wash dish
'Ban, 'Ban, Caliban
has a new master: get a
new man.
Freedom, hey-day! hey-
day, freedom! freedom,
hey-day, freedom!

STEPHANO

O brave monster!
Lead the way.

EXEUNT
FAST FADE

Before Prospero's cell.

ENTER Ferdinand, bearing a log

FERDINAND

There be some sports are
painful, and their
labour delight in them;
sets off some kinds of
baseness
are nobly undergone
and most poor matters
point to rich ends.
This my mean task

[places log on pile]
would be as heavy to me

as odious, but the
mistress which I serve
quickens what's dead
and makes my labours
pleasures:
O, she is ten times more
gentle than her father's
crabbed,
and he's composed of
harshness.
I must remove
some thousands of these
logs
and pile them up,
upon a sore injunction:
my sweet mistress weeps
when she sees me work,
and says, such baseness
had never like executor.
I forget:
but these sweet thoughts
do even refresh my
labours,
most busy lest, when I
do it.

ENTER MIRANDA; and PROSPERO at a distance, unseen

MIRANDA

Alas, now, pray you,
work not so hard:
I would the lightning
had
burnt up those logs
that you are enjoin'd to
pile!
Pray, set it down and
rest you: when this
burns, 'twill weep
for having wearied you.
My father is hard at
study;
pray now, rest yourself;
he's safe for these
three hours.

FERDINAND

O most dear mistress,
the sun will set
before I shall discharge

what I must strive to
do.

MIRANDA

If you'll sit down,
I'll bear your logs the
while: pray, give me
that;
I'll carry it to the
pile.

FERDINAND

No, precious creature;
I had rather crack my
sinews,
break my back, than you
should such dishonour
undergo,
while I sit lazy by.

MIRANDA

It would become me
as well as it does you:
and I should do it
with much more ease;
for my good will is to
it,
and yours it is against.

PROSPERO

Poor worm,
thou art infected!
This visitation shows
it.

MIRANDA

You look wearily.

FERDINAND

No, noble mistress;
'tis fresh morning
with me
when you are
by at night.
I do beseech you--
chiefly that I might set
it in my prayers--

what is your name?

                    MIRANDA

Miranda--O my father,
I have broke your hest
to say so!

                    FERDINAND

Admired Miranda!
Indeed the top of
admiration worth
what's dearest to the
world!
Full many a lady I have
eyed
with best regard and
many a time
the harmony of their
tongues
hath into bondage
brought my too diligent
ear:
for several virtues
have I liked several
women;
never any with so fun
soul,
but some defect in her
did quarrel with the
noblest grace she owed
and put it to the foil:
but you, O you,
so perfect and so
peerless,
are created
of every creature's
best!

                    MIRANDA

I do not know one
of my sex;
no woman's face
remember,
save, from my glass,
mine own;
nor have I seen
more that I may call men
than you, good friend,
and my dear father: how

features are abroad,
I am skilless of;
but, by my modesty,
the jewel in my dower,
I would not wish
any companion in the
world but you,
nor can imagination
form a shape,
besides yourself,
to like of.
but I prattle something
too wildly and my
father's precepts
I therein do forget.

FERDINAND

I am in my condition
a prince, Miranda;
I do think, a king;
I would, not so!--
and would no more endure
this wooden slavery
than to suffer
the flesh-fly blow my
mouth.
hear my soul speak:
the very instant that I
saw you, did my heart
fly to your service;
there resides,
to make me slave to it;
and for your sake
am I this patient log-
man.

MIRANDA

Do you love me?

FERDINAND

O heaven, O earth,
bear witness to this
sound
and crown what I profess
with kind event if I
speak true!
If hollowly, invert what
best is boded me to
mischief!

I beyond all limit
of what else i' the
world
o love, prize, honour
you.

MIRANDA

I am a fool
to weep at what I am
glad of.

PROSPERO

Fair encounter
of two most rare
affections!
Heavens rain grace
on that which breeds
between 'em!

FERDINAND

Wherefore weep you?

MIRANDA

At mine unworthiness
that dare not offer
what I desire to give,
and much less take
what I shall die to
want.
But this is trifling;
and all the more
it seeks to hide itself,
the bigger bulk it
shows.
Hence, bashful cunning!
and prompt me,
plain and holy
innocence!
I am your wife,
if you will marry me;
if not,
I'll die your maid:
to be your fellow
you may deny me;
but I'll be your
servant,
whether you will or no.

                    FERDINAND

          My mistress, dearest;
          and I thus humble ever.

                    MIRANDA

          My husband, then?

                    FERDINAND

          Ay, with a heart as
          willing
          as bondage e'er of
          freedom:
          here's my hand.

                    MIRANDA

          and mine, with my heart
          in't;
          and now farewell
          till half an hour hence.

                    FERDINAND

          A thousand thousand!

EXEUNT FERDINAND and MIRANDA severally

                    PROSPERO

          So glad of this
          as they I cannot be,
          who are surprised
          withal;
          but my rejoicing
          at nothing can be more.
          I'll to my book,
          for yet ere supper-time
          must I perform
          much business
          appertaining.

EXIT

                                        FAST FADE

Another part of the island.

ENTER CALIBAN, STEPHANO, and TRINCULO

STEPHANO

Tell not me; when the
butt is out, we will
drink water;
not a drop before:
therefore bear up, and
board 'em. Servant-
monster, drink to me.

Hands the bottle to Caliban

TRINCULO

Servant-monster!
the folly of this
island!
They say there's but
five upon this isle:
we are three
of them; if th'other two
be brained like us,
the state totters.

STEPHANO

Drink, servant-monster,
when I bid thee: thy
eyes are almost set in
thy head.

Caliban drinks from the bottle

TRINCULO

Where should they be set
else?
he were a brave monster
indeed,
if they were set in his
tail.

STEPHANO

My man-monster hath
drown'd
his tongue in sack:
for my part,
the sea cannot drown me;
I swam, ere I could
recover the shore,
five and thirty leagues
off and on.

By this light,
thou shalt be my
lieutenant,
monster, or my standard.

TRINCULO

Your lieutenant,
if you list;
he's no standard.

STEPHANO

We'll not run, Monsieur
Monster.

TRINCULO

Nor go neither;
but you'll lie like dogs
and yet say nothing
neither.

STEPHANO

Moon-calf, speak once in
thy life, if thou beest
a good moon-calf.

CALIBAN

How does thy honour?
Let me lick thy shoe.
I'll not serve him;
he's not valiant.

TRINCULO

Thou liest, most
ignorant monster: I am
in case to justle a
constable.
Why, thou deboshed fish
thou,
was there ever man a
coward
that hath drunk so much
sack as I to-day?
Wilt thou tell a
monstrous lie,
being but half a fish
and half a monster?

CALIBAN

Lo, how he mocks me!
wilt thou let him, my
lord?

TRINCULO

'Lord' quoth he! That a
monster should be such a
natural!

CALIBAN

Lo, lo, again! bite him
to death, I prithee.

STEPHANO

Trinculo,
keep a good tongue in
your head:
if you prove a
mutineer,--
the next tree!
The poor monster's my
subject
and he shall not suffer
indignity.

CALIBAN

I thank my noble lord.
Wilt thou be pleased to
hearken once again
to the suit I made to
thee?

STEPHANO

Marry, will I kneel and
repeat it; I will stand,
and so shall Trinculo.

ENTER ARIEL, invisible

CALIBAN

As I told thee before,
I am subject
to a tyrant,
a sorcerer, that by his
cunning hath cheated me

of the island.

ARIEL

Thou liest.

CALIBAN

Thou liest, thou jesting
monkey, thou: I would my
valiant master would
destroy thee! I do not
lie.

STEPHANO

Trinculo,
if you trouble him any
more
in's tale, by this hand,
I will supplant some of
your teeth.

TRINCULO

Why, I said nothing.

STEPHANO

Mum, then, and no more.
Proceed.

CALIBAN

I say, by sorcery
he got this isle;
from me he got it.
if thy greatness will
revenge it on him, - for
I know thou darest, but
this thing dare not,-

STEPHANO

That's most certain.

CALIBAN

Thou shalt be lord of it
and I'll serve thee.

STEPHANO

How now shall this be
compassed?
Canst thou bring me to
the party?

CALIBAN

Yea, yea, my lord:
I'll yield him thee
asleep,
where thou mayst knock a
nail
into his head.

ARIEL

Thou liest;
thou canst not.

CALIBAN

What a pied ninny's
this!
Thou scurvy patch!
I do beseech thy
greatness,
give him blows
and take his bottle from
him:
when that's gone
he shall drink nought
but brine; for I'll not
show him
where the quick freshes
are.

STEPHANO

Trinculo,
run into no further
danger:
interrupt the monster
one word further, and,
by this hand,
I'll turn my mercy out
o' doors
and make a stock-fish of
thee.

TRINCULO

Why, what did I? I did
nothing. I'll go farther

off.

STEPHANO

Didst thou not say he
lied?

ARIEL

Thou liest.

STEPHANO

Do I so? Take thou that.

Beats TRINCULO

As you like this,
give me the lie another
time.

TRINCULO

I did not give the lie.
Out o' your wits and
bearing too?
A pox o' your bottle!
This can sack and
drinking do.
A murrain on your
monster,
and the devil take your
fingers!

CALIBAN

Ha, ha, ha!

STEPHANO

Now, forward with your
tale. Prithee, stand
farther off.

CALIBAN

Beat him enough:
after a little time
I'll beat him too.

STEPHANO

Stand farther.

Come, proceed.

CALIBAN

Why, as I told thee,
'tis a custom with him,
i' th' afternoon to
sleep:
there thou mayst brain
him,
having first seized his
books,
or with a log batter his
skull,
or paunch him with a
stake,
or cut his windpipe
with thy knife. Remember
first to possess his
books;
for without them he's
but a sot, as I am,
nor hath not one spirit
to command:
they all do hate him
as rootedly as I.
Burn but his books.
He has brave utensils,--
for so he calls them--
which when he has a
house,
he'll deck withal and
that most deeply to
consider
is the beauty of his
daughter;
he himself calls her a
nonpareil:
I never saw a woman,
but only Sycorax my dam
and she; but she as far
surpasseth Sycorax
as great'st does least.

STEPHANO

Is it so brave a lass?

CALIBAN

Ay, lord; she will
become thy bed,

I warrant.
And bring thee forth
brave brood.

STEPHANO

Monster, I will kill
this man:
his daughter and I
will be king and queen--
save our graces!--
and Trinculo and thyself
shall be viceroys.
Dost thou like the plot,
Trinculo?

TRINCULO

Excellent.

STEPHANO

shaking hands with Trinculo
Give me thy hand:
I am sorry I beat thee;
but,
while thou livest,
keep a good tongue in
thy head.

CALIBAN

Within this half hour
will he be asleep: wilt
thou destroy him then?

STEPHANO

Ay, on mine honour.

ARIEL

This will I tell my
master.

CALIBAN

Thou makest me merry;
I am full of pleasure:
let us be jocund:
will you troll the catch
you taught me but while-
ere?

STEPHANO

At thy request, monster,
I will do reason,
any reason.
Come on, Trinculo,
let us sing.

Sings

Flout 'em and scout 'em
And scout 'em and flout
'em.
Thought is free.

CALIBAN

That's not the tune.

Ariel plays the tune on a tabour and pipe

STEPHANO

What is this same?

TRINCULO

This is the tune of our
catch, played by the
picture of Nobody.

STEPHANO

If thou beest a man,
show thyself in thy
likeness:
if thou beest a devil,
take't as thou list.

TRINCULO

O, forgive me my sins!

STEPHANO

He that dies pays all
debts: I defy thee.
Mercy upon us!

CALIBAN

Art thou afeard?

STEPHANO

No, monster, not I.

CALIBAN

Be not afeard;
the isle is full of
noises,
sounds and sweet airs,
that give delight and
hurt not.
Sometimes
a thousand twangling
instruments
will hum about mine
ears,
and sometime voices
that, if I then had
waked
after long sleep,
will make me sleep
again:
and then, in dreaming,
the clouds methought
would open
and show riches
ready to drop upon me
that,
when I waked,
I cried to dream again.

STEPHANO

This will prove a brave
kingdom
to me, where I shall
have my music for
nothing.

CALIBAN

When Prospero is
destroyed.

STEPHANO

That shall be by and by:
I remember the story.

TRINCULO

The sound is going away;

let's follow it,
and after do our work.

STEPHANO

Lead, monster; we'll
follow.
I would I could see this
tabourer; he lays it on.

TRINCULO

Wilt come? I'll follow,
Stephano.

EXEUNT

FAST FADE

Another part of the island.

ENTER ALONSO, SEBASTIAN, ANTONIO, GONZALO,
ADRIAN, FRANCISCO, and others

GONZALO
By'r la'kin,
I can go no further,
sir;
my old bones ache:
here's a maze trod
indeed
through forth-rights and
meanders! By your
patience,
I needs must rest me.

ALONSO

Old lord, I cannot blame
thee,
who am myself
attach'd with weariness,
to the dulling of my
spirits:
sit down, and rest.

Gonzalo sits down

Even here I will put off
my hope and keep it
no longer for my
flatterer:
he is drown'd whom thus
we stray

to find, and the sea
mocks
our frustrate search on
land.
Well, let him go.

ANTONIO

[Aside to SEBASTIAN]

I am right glad
that he's so out of
hope.
Do not, for one repulse,
forego the purpose
that you resolved to
effect.

SEBASTIAN

[Aside to ANTONIO]

The next advantage will
we take throughly.

ANTONIO

[Aside to SEBASTIAN]

Let it be to-night;
for, now
they are oppress'd with
travel, they will not,
nor cannot,
use such vigilance
as when they are fresh.

SEBASTIAN

[Aside to ANTONIO]

I say, tonight: no more.

Solemn and strange music

ALONSO

What harmony is this?
My good friends, hark!

GONZALO

Marvellous sweet music!

ENTER PROSPERO above, invisible.

ENTER several strange Shapes, bringing in a
banquet; they dance about it with gentle actions
of salutation; and, inviting the King, & c. to
eat, they depart

ALONSO

Give us kind keepers,
heavens!
What were these?

SEBASTIAN

A living drollery.
Now I will believe
That there are unicorns,
that in Arabia there is
one tree, the phoenix'
throne,
one phoenix at this hour
reigning there.

ANTONIO

I'll believe both;
and what does else want
credit, come to me,
and I'll be sworn 'tis
true: travellers ne'er
did lie,
though fools at home
condemn 'em.

GONZALO

If in Naples I should
report this now, would
they believe me?
If I should say,
I saw such islanders--
for, certes,
these are people of the
island--
who, though they are of
monstrous shape, yet,
note,
their manners are more

gentle-kind than of our
human generation
you shall find
many, nay, almost any.

PROSPERO
[Aside]
Honest lord, thou hast
said well; for some of
you there present
are worse than devils.

ALONSO

I cannot too much muse
such shapes, such
gesture and such sound,
expressing, although
they want the use of
tongue,
a kind of excellent
dumb discourse.

PROSPERO
[Aside]
Praise in departing.

FRANCISCO

They vanish'd strangely.

SEBASTIAN

No matter, since
they have left their
viands behind; for we
have stomachs.
Will't please you taste
of what is here?

ALONSO

Not I.

GONZALO

Faith, sir,
you need not fear.
When we were boys,
who would believe that
there were mountaineers
dew-lapp'd like bulls,
whose throats had

hanging at 'em
wallets of flesh?
or that there were
such men whose heads
stood in their breasts?
Which now we find
each putter-out of five
for one will bring us
good warrant of.

ALONSO

I will stand to
and feed,
although my last:
no matter, since I feel
the best is past.
Brother, my lord the
duke,
stand to and do as we.

Thunder and lightning.

ENTER ARIEL, like a harpy; claps his wings upon
the table; and, with a quaint device, the banquet
vanishes

ARIEL

You are three men of
sin, whom Destiny,
that hath to instrument
this lower world
and what is in't,
the never-surfeited sea
hath caused to belch up
you; and on this island
where man doth not
inhabit; you 'mongst men
being most unfit
to live.
I have made you mad;
and even with such-like
valour
men hang and drown
their proper selves.

ALONSO, SEBASTIAN & c. draw their swords
You fools! I and my
fellows
are ministers of Fate:
the elements,

of whom your swords are
temper'd, may as well
wound the loud winds, or
with bemock'd-at stabs
kill the still-closing
waters,
as diminish one dowle
that's in my plume:
my fellow-ministers
are like invulnerable.
If you could hurt,
your swords are now too
massy
for your strengths
and will not be
uplifted.
But remember--
for that's my business
to you--
that you three
from Milan
did supplant good
Prospero;
exposed unto the sea,
which hath requit it,
him and his innocent
child:
for which foul deed
the powers, delaying,
not forgetting,
have incensed the seas
and shores, yea,
all the creatures,
against your peace.
thee of thy son, Alonso,
they have bereft;
and do pronounce by me:
lingering perdition,
worse than any death
can be at once,
shall step by step
attend you
and your ways;
whose wraths to guard
you from-which here, in
this most desolate isle,
else falls upon your
heads-
is nothing but heart-
sorrow and a clear life
ensuing.

He vanishes in thunder; then, to soft music enter
the Shapes again, and dance, with mocks and mows,
and carrying out the table

PROSPERO

Bravely the figure of
this harpy hast thou
perform'd, my Ariel;
a grace it had,
devouring:
of my instruction
hast thou nothing bated
in what thou hadst to
say: so, with good life
and observation strange,
my meaner ministers
their several kinds
have done.
My high charms work
and these mine enemies
are all knit up
in their distractions;
they now are in my
power; and in these fits
I leave them, while I
visit young Ferdinand,
whom they suppose is
drown'd,
and his and mine loved
darling.

EXIT above

GONZALO

I' the name of something
holy,
Sir, why stand you
in this strange stare?

ALONSO

O, it is monstrous,
monstrous:
methought the billows
spoke
and told me of it;
the winds did sing it to
me, and the thunder,
that deep and dreadful
organ-pipe, pronounced
The name of Prosper:

it did bass my trespass.
Therefore my son
i' the ooze is bedded,
and I'll seek him deeper
than e'er plummet
sounded
and with him there lie
mudded.

EXIT

SEBASTIAN

But one fiend at a time,
I'll fight their legions
o'er.

ANTONIO

I'll be thy second.

EXEUNT SEBASTIAN, and ANTONIO swords drawn

GONZALO

All three of them
are desperate:
their great guilt,
like poison
given to work
a great time after,
now 'gins to bite the
spirits.
I do beseech you
that are of suppler
joints,
follow them swiftly
and hinder them from
what this ecstasy
may now provoke them to.

ADRIAN

Follow, I pray you.
EXEUNT
                                                FADES
Before PROSPERO'S cell.

ENTER PROSPERO, FERDINAND, and MIRANDA

PROSPERO

If I have too austerely

punish'd you,
your compensation
makes amends,
for I have given you
here a third
of mine own life,
or that for which I
live; who once again
I tender to thy hand:
all thy vexations
were but my trials of
thy love
and thou hast strangely
stood the test here,
afore Heaven,
I ratify this
my rich gift.
Ferdinand, do not smile
at me
that I boast her off,
for thou shalt find she
will outstrip all praise
and make it halt behind
her.

FERDINAND

I do believe it against
an oracle.

PROSPERO

Then, as my gift
and thine own
acquisition
worthily purchased,
take my daughter:
but if thou dost break
her virgin-knot before
all sanctifying
ceremonies
may with full and holy
rite
be minister'd,
no sweet aspersion
shall the heavens let
fall
to make this contract
grow: but barren hate,
sour-eyed disdain and
discord
shall bestrew the union

of your bed with weeds
so loathly
that you shall hate it
both: therefore take
heed, as Hymen's lamps
shall light you.

FERDINAND

As I hope for quiet
days, fair issue
and long life,
with such love as
'tis now,
the murkiest den,
the most opportune
place,
the strong'st
suggestion.
our worser genius can,
shall never melt
mine honour into lust,
to take away the edge
of that day's
celebration
when I shall think:
or Phoebus' steeds are
founder'd, or Night kept
chain'd below.

PROSPERO

Fairly spoke.
Sit then and talk with
her;
she is thine own.
What, Ariel!
my industrious servant,
Ariel!

ENTER ARIEL

ARIEL

What would my potent
master? Here I am.

PROSPERO

Thou and thy meaner
fellows
your last service did
worthily perform;

and I must use you
in such another trick.
Go bring the rabble,
o'er whom I give thee
power,
here to this place:
incite them to quick
motion;
for I must bestow upon
the eyes
of this young couple
some vanity of mine art:
it is my promise,
and they expect it from
me.

             ARIEL

Presently?

             PROSPERO

ARIEL (sings)

Ay, with a twink.
Before you can say
'come' and 'go,'
and breathe twice and
cry
'so, so,'
each one, tripping on
his toe,
will be here with mop
and mow.
Do you love me, master?
No?

             PROSPERO

Dearly my delicate
Ariel.
Do not approach till
thou dost hear me call.

             ARIEL

Well, I conceive.

EXIT

             PROSPERO

Look thou be true;

do not give dalliance
too much the rein:
the strongest oaths are
straw
to the fire i' the
blood:
be more abstemious,
or else, good night your
vow!

                    FERDINAND

I warrant you sir;
the white cold virgin
snow
upon my heart abates
the ardour of my liver.

                    PROSPERO

Well! Now come my Ariel;
bring a corollary
rather than want a
spirit.
Appear, and pertly.
Soft music
No tongue, all eyes. Be
silent

Enter certain Nymphs
('Gypsy'/Asian, naked and barefoot, but wearing
sleeved, long diaphanous gowns)
followed by certain Reapers, properly habited.
(As Manx teuchtars they all wear carranes. Each
carries a sickle with golden hook. They join
with the Nymphs in a graceful dance (Sitar,
blues harp and bodhran drum); towards the end
whereof Prospero starts suddenly and speaks;
after which, to a strange hollow and confused
noise, they heavily vanish.

                PROSPERO (aside) (CONT'D)

I had forgot that foul
conspiracy
of the beast Caliban
and his confederates
against my life:
the minute of their plot
is almost come.

                FERDINAND (To Miranda)

This is strange:
your father's in some
passion
that works him strongly.

MIRANDA

Never till this day
saw I him touch'd
with anger so
distemper'd.

PROSPERO

You do look, my son,
in a moved sort,
as if you were dismay'd:
be cheerful, sir.
Our revels
now are ended.
These our actors,
As I foretold you, were
all spirits and are
melted into air,
into thin air:
and, like the baseless
fabric of this vision,
the cloud-capp'd towers,
the gorgeous palaces,
the solemn temples,
the great globe itself,
yea all which it
inherit,
shall dissolve, and like
this insubstantial
pageant faded,
leave not a rack behind.
We are such stuff
as dreams are made on,
and our little life
is rounded with a sleep.
Sir, I am vex'd;
bear with my weakness;
my, brain is troubled:
be not disturb'd with my
infirmity:
if you be pleased,
retire into my cell
and there repose: a turn
or two I'll walk,
to still my beating

mind.

FERDINAND and MIRANDA

We wish your peace.

EXEUNT

PROSPERO

Come with a thought I
thank thee, Ariel: come.

ENTER ARIEL

ARIEL

Thy thoughts I cleave
to. What's thy pleasure?

PROSPERO

Spirit, we must prepare
to meet with Caliban.

ARIEL

Ay, my commander:
I thought to have told
thee of it, but I fear'd
lest I might anger thee.

PROSPERO

Say again, where didst
thou leave these
varlets?

ARIEL

I told you, sir,
they were red-hot with
drinking;
so full of valour
that they smote the air
For breathing in their
faces;
beat the ground
for kissing of their
feet;
yet always bending
towards their project.
Then I beat my tabour;

at which, like unback'd
colts,
they prick'd their ears,
advanced their eyelids,
lifted up their noses
as they smelt music:
so I charm'd their ears
that calf-like they my
lowing follow'd through
tooth'd briers, sharp
furzes, pricking goss
and thorns, which
entered
their frail shins:
at last I left them
i' the filthy-mantled
pool beyond your cell,
there dancing
up to the chins,
that the foul lake
o'erstunk their feet.

PROSPERO

This was well done,
my bird.
Thy shape invisible
retain thou still:
the trumpery
in my house,
go bring it hither,
for stale to catch these
thieves.

ARIEL

I go, I go.

EXIT

PROSPERO

A devil, a born devil,
on whose nature
nurture can never stick;
on whom my pains,
humanely taken,
all, all lost, quite
lost; and as with age
his body uglier grows,
so his mind cankers.
I will plague them all,
even to roaring.

RE-ENTER ARIEL, loaden with glistering apparel.

> Come, hang them on this
> line.

Ariel arranges the gaudy and zany clothing on the
line

PROSPERO and ARIEL remain invisible. ENTER
CALIBAN, STEPHANO, and TRINCULO, all wet

CALIBAN

> Pray you, tread softly,
> that the blind mole may
> not hear a foot fall:
> we now are near his
> cell.

STEPHANO

> Monster, your fairy,
> which you say is a
> harmless fairy, has done
> little better than
> played the Jack with us.

TRINCULO

> Monster, I do smell all
> horse-piss;
> at which my nose
> is in great indignation.

STEPHANO

> So is mine. Do you hear,
> monster? If I should
> take a displeasure
> against you, look you,--

TRINCULO

> Thou wert but a lost
> monster.

CALIBAN

> Good my lord, give me
> thy favour still.
> Be patient, for the
> prize I'll bring thee to
> shall hoodwink this

mischance: therefore
speak softly.
All's hush'd as midnight
yet.

                    TRINCULO

Ay, but to lose our
bottles in the pool,--

                    STEPHANO

There is not only
disgrace and dishonour
in that, monster,
but an infinite loss.

                    TRINCULO

That's more to me than
my wetting: yet this is
your harmless fairy,
monster.

                    STEPHANO

I will fetch off my
bottle,
though I be o'er ears
for my labour.

                    CALIBAN

Prithee, my king, be
quiet.
Seest thou here,
This is the mouth o' the
cell:
no noise, and enter.
Do that good mischief
which may make this
island
thine own for ever,
and I, thy Caliban,
for aye thy foot-licker.

                    STEPHANO

Give me thy hand.
I do begin to have
bloody thoughts.

TRINCULO

O king Stephano! O peer!
O worthy Stephano!
Look what a wardrobe
here is for thee!

CALIBAN

Let it alone, thou fool;
it is but trash.

TRINCULO

[Starts putting on fancy dress]
O, ho, monster!
we know what belongs to
a frippery.
O king Stephano!

STEPHANO

Put off that gown,
Trinculo;
by this hand,
I'll have that gown.

TRINCULO

Thy grace shall have it.

CALIBAN

The dropsy drown this
fool.
What do you mean
to dote thus on such
luggage?
Let's along
and do the murder first:
if he awake, from toe to
crown he'll fill our
skins with pinches,
make us strange stuff.

STEPHANO

Be you quiet, monster.
Mistress line,
is not this my jerkin?
Now is the jerkin under
the line: now, jerkin,

you are like to lose
your hair
and prove a bald jerkin.

[Stephano tries on a fancy jerkin]

                TRINCULO

Do, do: we steal by line
and level, an't like
your grace.

                STEPHANO

I thank thee for that
jest;
here's a garment for't:

[He hands Trinculo another item off the line]

it shall not go
unrewarded
while I am king
of this country.
'Steal by line and
level'
is an excellent pass of
pate; there's another
garment for't.

                TRINCULO

Monster, come, put some
lime
upon your fingers,
and away with the rest.

                CALIBAN

I will have none on't:
we shall lose our time,
and all be turn'd to
barnacles, or to apes
with foreheads
villainous low.

                STEPHANO

Away where my hogshead
of wine is, or I'll turn
you out of my kingdom:
go to, carry this.

TRINCULO

And this.

STEPHANO

Ay, and this.

[They hand more clothes to Caliban]

A noise of hunters heard. ENTER divers Spirits,
in shape of dogs and hounds, and hunt them about,
PROSPERO and ARIEL setting them on [minimum 4
Basset hounds]

PROSPERO

Hey, Mountain, hey!

ARIEL

Silver! There it goes,
Silver!

PROSPERO

Fury, Fury! There,
Tyrant, there! Hark!
Hark!

CALIBAN, STEPHANO, and TRINCULO, are driven out

Go charge my goblins
that they grind their
joints
with dry convulsions,
shorten up their sinews
with aged cramps,
and more pinch-spotted
make them than pard
or cat o' mountain.

ARIEL

Hark, they roar!

PROSPERO

Let them be hunted
soundly.
At this hour
lie at my mercy all mine
enemies:

shortly shall all my
labours end, and thou
shalt have the air at
freedom:
for a little follow,
and do me service.

                              EXEUNT
                         FAST FADE

Before PROSPERO'S cell.

ENTER PROSPERO in his magic robes, and ARIEL

                PROSPERO

        Now does my project
        gather to a head:
        my charms crack not;
        my spirits obey;
        and time
        goes upright with his
        carriage. How's the day?

                ARIEL

        On the sixth hour;
        at which time, my lord,
        you said our work should
        cease.

                PROSPERO

        I did say so,
        when first I raised the
        tempest.
        Ay, my spirit,
        how fares the king
        and's followers?

                ARIEL

        Confined together in the
        same fashion as you gave
        in charge,
        just as you left them;
        all prisoners, sir,
        in the line-grove
        which weather-fends your
        cell;
        they cannot budge
        till your release.
        The king, his brother
        and yours, abide all

three distracted
and the remainder
mourning over them,
brimful of sorrow and
dismay;
but chiefly him that you
term'd, sir, 'the good
old lord Gonzalo;'
his tears run down his
beard,
like winter's drops
from eaves of reeds.
Your charm so strongly
works 'em
that if you now beheld
them,
your affections
would become tender.

PROSPERO

Dost thou think so,
spirit?

ARIEL

Mine would, sir, were I
human.

PROSPERO

And mine shall.
Hast thou,
which art but air,
a touch, a feeling
of their afflictions,
and shall not myself,
one of their kind,
that relish all as
sharply,
passion as they,
be kindlier moved than
thou art?
Though with their high
wrongs
I am struck to the
quick,
yet with my nobler
reason
'gainst my fury do I
take part:
the rarer action is

in virtue than in
vengeance:
they being penitent,
the sole drift of my
purpose
doth extend not a frown
further.
Go release them, Ariel:
my charms I'll break,
their senses I'll
restore,
and they shall be
themselves.

ARIEL

I'll fetch them, sir.

EXIT

PROSPERO

Ye elves of hills,
brooks, standing lakes
and groves,
and ye that on the sands
with printless foot
do chase the ebbing
Neptune
and do fly him when he
comes back; you demi-
puppets that by
moonshine do the green
sour ringlets make,
whereof the ewe not
bites,
and you whose pastime
is to make midnight
mushrooms,
that rejoice to hear
the solemn curfew; by
whose aid,
weak masters though ye
be,
I have bedimm'd the
noontide sun, call'd
forth the mutinous
winds,
and 'twixt the green sea
and the azured vault
set roaring war:
to the dread rattling

thunder
have I given fire and
rifted Jove's stout oak
with his own bolt;
the strong-based
promontory
have I made shake
and by the spurs pluck'd
up the pine and cedar:
graves at my command
have waked their
sleepers,
oped, and let 'em forth
by my so potent art.
But this rough magic
I here abjure,
and, when I have
required
some heavenly music,
which even now I do,
to work mine
end upon their senses
that this airy charm is
for,
I'll break my staff,
Bury it certain fathoms
in the earth, And deeper
than did ever plummet
sound
I'll drown my book.

Solemn music

RE-ENTER ARIEL before: then ALONSO, with a
frantic gesture, attended by GONZALO; SEBASTIAN
and ANTONIO in like manner, attended by ADRIAN
and FRANCISCO they all enter the circle which
PROSPERO had made, and there stand charmed; which
PROSPERO observing, speaks:

                    PROSPERO (CONT'D)

A solemn air and the
best comforter

[Music continues]

to an unsettled fancy
cure thy brains,
now useless,
boil'd within thy skull!
There stand,

for you are spell-
stopp'd.
holy Gonzalo,
honourable man,
mine eyes, even sociable
to the show of thine,
fall fellowly drops.
The charm dissolves
apace,
and as the morning
steals upon the night,
melting the darkness,
so their rising senses
begin to chase the
ignorant fumes that
mantle their clearer
reason.
O good Gonzalo,
my true preserver,
and a loyal sir
to him you follow'st!
I will pay thy graces
home
both in word and deed.
Most cruelly didst thou,
Alonso, use me and my
daughter:
thy brother was a
furtherer in the act.
Thou art pinch'd fort
now, Sebastian.
Flesh and blood,
you, brother mine,
that entertain'd
ambition,
expell'd remorse and
nature; who, with
Sebastian,
whose inward pinches
therefore are most
strong,
would here have kill'd
your king;
I do forgive thee,
unnatural though thou
art.
Their understanding
begins to swell,
and the approaching tide
will shortly fill
the reasonable shore
that now lies foul and

muddy. Not one of them
that yet looks on me,
or would know me Ariel,
fetch me the hat and
rapier in my cell:
I will discase me,
and myself present
as I was sometime Milan:
quickly, spirit; thou
shalt ere long be free.

ARIEL sings and helps to attire him

ARIEL

Where the bee sucks.
there suck I:
in a cowslip's bell I
lie;
there I couch when owls
do cry.
On the bat's back I do
fly
after summer merrily.
Merrily, merrily shall I
live now
under the blossom
that hangs on the bough.

PROSPERO

Why, that's my dainty
Ariel!
I shall miss thee:
but yet thou shalt have
freedom: so, so, so.
To the king's ship,
invisible as thou art:
There shalt thou find
the mariners asleep
under the hatches;
the master and the
boatswain being awake,
enforce them to this
place, and presently,
I prithee.

ARIEL

I drink the air
before me, and return or
ere your pulse twice
beat.

EXIT

GONZALO

All torment, trouble,
wonder
and amazement inhabits
here:
some heavenly power
guide us
out of this fearful
country!

PROSPERO

Behold, sir king,
the wronged Duke of
Milan, Prospero:
for more assurance that
a living prince does now
speak to thee,
I embrace thy body;
and to thee and thy
company
I bid a hearty welcome.

ALONSO

Whether thou best
he or no,
or some enchanted trifle
to abuse me, as late I
have been, I not know:
thy pulse beats
as of flesh and blood;
and, since I saw thee,
the affliction of my
mind amends, with which,
I fear,
a madness held me:
this must crave,
and if this be at all,
a most strange story.
Thy dukedom I resign
and do entreat
thou pardon me my
wrongs.
But how should Prospero
be living and be here?

PROSPERO

First, noble friend,
let me embrace thine
age, whose honour cannot
be measured or confined.

GONZALO

Whether this be or be
not, I'll not swear.

PROSPERO

You do yet taste
some subtilties o' the
isle,
that will not let you
believe things certain.
Welcome, my friends all!

(Aside to SEBASTIAN and ANTONIO)
But you, my brace of
lords,
were I so minded,
I here could pluck
his highness' frown upon
you
and justify you
traitors: at this time
I will tell no tales.

SEBASTIAN [Aside]
The devil speaks in him.

PROSPERO (CONT'D)
No. For you, most wicked
sir,
whom to call brother
would even infect my
mouth,
I do forgive thy rankest
fault; all of them;
and require my dukedom
of thee, which perforce,
I know,
thou must restore.

ALONSO

If thou be'st Prospero,
give us particulars
of thy preservation;

how thou hast met us
here,
who three hours since
were wreck'd upon this
shore;
where I have lost--
how sharp the point of
this remembrance is!--
my dear son Ferdinand.

PROSPERO

I am woe for't, sir.

ALONSO

Irreparable is the loss,
and patience says it is
past her cure.

PROSPERO

I rather think you have
not sought her help,
of whose soft grace
for the like loss
I have her sovereign aid
and rest myself content.

ALONSO

You the like loss!

PROSPERO

As great to me as late;
and, supportable
to make the dear loss,
have I means much weaker
than you may call to
comfort you, for I have
lost my daughter.

ALONSO

A daughter? O heavens,
that they were living
both in Naples,
the king and queen
there!
that they were, I wish
myself were mudded
in that oozy bed

where my son lies.
When did you lose your
daughter?

PROSPERO

In this last tempest.
I perceive these lords
at this encounter
do so much admire
that they devour their
reason
and scarce think
their eyes do offices of
truth, their words are
natural breath: but,
howsoe'er you have
been justled
from your senses,
know for certain that I
am Prospero
and that very duke
which was thrust forth
of Milan, who most
strangely
upon this shore,
where you were wreck'd,
was landed, to be the
lord on't.
No more yet of this;
for 'tis a chronicle
of day by day,
not a relation for a
breakfast nor
befitting this first
meeting. Welcome, sir;
this cell's my court:
here have I few
attendants
and subjects none
abroad:
pray you, look in.
My dukedom
since you have given me
again,
I will requite you
with as good a thing;
at least bring forth a
wonder, to content ye
as much as me my
dukedom.

Here PROSPERO discovers FERDINAND and MIRANDA
playing at chess

                        MIRANDA

        Sweet lord, you play me
        false.

                        FERDINAND

        No, my dear'st love,
        I would not for the
        world.

                        MIRANDA

        Yes, for a score of
        kingdoms
        you should wrangle,
        And I would call it,
        fair play.

                        ALONSO

        If this prove
        a vision of the island,
        one dear son shall I
        twice lose.

                        SEBASTIAN

        A most high miracle!

                        FERDINAND

        Though the seas
        threaten,
        they are merciful;
        I have cursed them
        without cause.

Kneels

                        ALONSO

        Now all the blessings
        of a glad father
        compass thee about!
        Arise,
        and say how thou camest
        here.

MIRANDA

O, wonder!
How many goodly
creatures
are there here!
How beauteous mankind
is! O brave new world,
that has such people
in't!

PROSPERO

'Tis new to thee.

ALONSO

What is this maid
with whom thou wast at
play?
Your eld'st acquaintance
cannot be three hours:
is she the goddess
that hath sever'd us,
and brought us thus
together?

FERDINAND

Sir, she is mortal;
but by immortal
Providence
she's mine:
I chose her
when I could not ask my
father
for his advice,
nor thought I had one.
She is daughter
to this famous Duke of
Milan, of whom so often
I have heard renown,
but never saw before;
of whom I have received
a second life; and
second father this lady
makes him to me.

ALONSO

I am hers:
but, O, how oddly will
it sound that I must ask

my child forgiveness!

PROSPERO

There, sir, stop:
Let us not burthen our
remembrance with a
heaviness that's gone.

GONZALO

I have inly wept,
Or should have spoke ere
this.
Look down, you god,
and on this couple
drop a blessed crown!
For it is you
that have chalk'd forth
the way
which brought us hither.

ALONSO

I say, Amen, Gonzalo!

GONZALO

Was Milan thrust from
Milan,
that his issue should
become kings of Naples?
O, rejoice
beyond a common joy,
and set it down
with gold on lasting
pillars:
in one voyage did
Claribel
her husband find at
Tunis,
and Ferdinand,
her brother,
found a wife
where he himself was
lost,
Prospero his dukedom
in a poor isle
and all of us ourselves
when no man was his own.

ALONSO

[To FERDINAND and
MIRANDA]
Give me your hands:
let grief and sorrow
still embrace his heart
that doth not wish you
joy!

GONZALO

Be it so! Amen!

Re-enter ARIEL, with the Master and Boatswain
amazedly following

O, look, sir, look, sir!
here is more of us: I
prophesied, if a gallows
were on land,
this fellow could not
drown.
Now, blasphemy,
that swear'st grace
o'erboard,
not an oath on shore?
Hast thou no mouth by
land? What is the news?

BOATSWAIN

The best news is,
that we have safely
found
our king and company;
the next, our ship--
which, but three glasses
since,
we gave out split--
is tight and yare
and bravely rigg'd
as when we first put out
to sea.

ARIEL [Aside to PROSPERO]

Sir, all this service
have I done since I
went.

PROSPERO [Aside to ARIEL]

My tricksy spirit!

ALONSO

These are not natural
events;
they strengthen
from strange to
stranger.
Say, how came you
hither?

BOATSWAIN

If I did think, sir,
I were well awake,
I'ld strive to tell you.
We were dead of sleep,
and--how we know not--
all clapp'd under
hatches;
where but even now
with strange and several
noises
of roaring, shrieking,
howling, jingling
chains,
and more diversity of
sounds, all horrible,
we were awaked;
straightway,
at liberty;
where we, in all her
trim, freshly beheld
our royal, good and
gallant ship, our master
capering to eye her:
on a trice, so please
you, even in a dream,
were we divided from
them
and were brought moping
hither.

ARIEL [Aside to PROSPERO]

Was't well done?

PROSPERO [Aside to ARIEL]

Bravely, my diligence.

Thou shalt be free.

ALONSO

This is as strange a
maze as e'er men trod
and there is in this
business
more than nature
was ever conduct of:
some oracle
must rectify our
knowledge.

PROSPERO

Sir, my liege,
do not infest your mind
with beating on
the strangeness of this
business; at pick'd
leisure
which shall be shortly,
single I'll resolve you,
which to you shall seem
probable, of every these
happen'd accidents; till
when, be cheerful
And think of each thing
well.

Aside to ARIEL

Come hither, spirit:
set Caliban
and his companions free;
untie the spell.

EXIT ARIEL

How fares my gracious
sir?
There are yet missing
of your company some few
odd lads that you
remember not.

RE-ENTER ARIEL, driving in CALIBAN, STEPHANO and
TRINCULO, in their stolen apparel

STEPHANO

Every man shift for all
the rest, and let no man
take care for himself;
for all is but fortune.
Coragio, bully-monster,
coragio!

TRINCULO

If these be true spies
which I wear in my head,
here's a goodly sight.

CALIBAN

O Setebos,
these be brave spirits
indeed!
How fine my master is!
I am afraid he will
chastise me.

SEBASTIAN
Ha, ha!
What things are these,
my lord Antonio?
Will money buy 'em?

ANTONIO

Very like;
one of them is a plain
fish, and, no doubt,
marketable.

PROSPERO

Mark but the badges of
these men, my lords,
then say if they be
true. This mis-shapen
knave,
his mother was a witch,
and one so strong

[INSET Sycorax grimacing and cursing]
that could control the
moon,
make flows and ebbs,
and deal in her command

without her power.
These three have robb'd
me; and this demi-devil-
for he's a bastard one-
had plotted with them
to take my life.
Two of these fellows you
must know and own;
this thing of darkness!
Acknowledge mine.

CALIBAN

I shall be pinch'd to
death.

ALONSO

Is not this Stephano,
my drunken butler?

SEBASTIAN

He is drunk now:
where had he wine?

ALONSO

And Trinculo is reeling
ripe:
where should they find
this grand liquor that
hath gilded 'em?
How camest thou in this
pickle?

TRINCULO

I have been in such a
pickle
since I saw you last
that, I fear me,
will never out of my
bones:
I shall not fear fly-
blowing.

SEBASTIAN

Why, how now, Stephano!

STEPHANO

O, touch me not;
I am not Stephano, but a
cramp.

PROSPERO

You'ld be king o'the
isle, sirrah?

STEPHANO

I should have been a
sore one then.

ALONSO Pointing to Caliban

This is a strange thing
as e'er I look'd on.

PROSPERO

He is as disproportion'd
in his manners as in his
shape.
Go, sirrah, to my cell;
take with you your
companions;
as you look to have my
pardon,
trim it handsomely.

CALIBAN

Ay, that I will;
and I'll be wise
hereafter
and seek for grace.
What a thrice-double ass
was I,
to take this drunkard
for a god
and worship this dull
fool!

PROSPERO

Go to; away!

ALONSO

Hence, and bestow your

luggage where you found
it.

SEBASTIAN

Or stole it, rather.

EXEUNT CALIBAN, STEPHANO, and TRINCULO

PROSPERO

Sir, I invite your
highness
and your train to my
poor cell,
where you shall take
your rest
for this one night;
which, part of it,
I'll waste with such
discourse as, I not
doubt, shall make it
go quick away;
the story of my life
and the particular
accidents
gone by since I came to
this isle: and in the
morn I'll bring you
to your ship and so to
Naples,
where I have hope to see
the nuptial of these our
dear-beloved solemnized;
and thence retire me to
my Milan, where every
third thought shall be
my grave.

ALONSO

I long to hear
the story of your life,
which must take the ear
strangely.

PROSPERO

I'll deliver all;
and promise you calm
seas, auspicious gales
and sail so expeditious
that shall catch your

  152

                    royal fleet far off.

                        (Aside to ARIEL)
                    My Ariel, chick,
                    that is thy charge: then
                    to the elements be free,
                    and fare thou well
                    Please you, draw near.
         EXEUNT

                                              FADES

         EPILOGUE spoken BY PROSPERO:

         [Image of Shakespeare Inset]
                    Now my charms are all
                    o'erthrown;
                    What strength I have's
                    mine own,
                    which is most faint:
                    now,tis true,
                    I must be here confined
                    by you,
                    or sent to Naples.
                    Let me not,
                    since I have my dukedom
                    got,
                    and pardon'd the
                    deceiver, dwell
                    in this bare island by
                    your spell,
                    but release me from my
                    bands
                    with the help of your
                    good hands:

         [mimes clapping]
                    gentle breath of yours
                    my sails
                    must fill
                    or else my project
                    fails,
                    which was to please.
                    Now I want spirits to
                    enforce,
                    art to enchant,
                    or my ending is despair,
                    unless I be relieved by
                    prayer,

         [mimes hands at prayer]
                    which pierces, so that
                    it assaults

        Mercy itself,
        and frees all faults.
        As you from crimes w'd
        pardon'd be,

[mimes begging]
        let your indulgence set
        me free.
[mimes clapping]

                                        FADES
                SCREEN TEXT:
Shakespeare returned to London in 1592, where he
lodged with a French Protestant refugee. He then
produced his series of masterpieces. His last
play before retirement was 'The Tempest', written
in 1610-1611, with first performance that year.
In it he has considered, through Prospero and
Ariel, the magic of the theatre and the
dramatist's art, and makes his own difficult
farewell to his audiences.

The Isle of Man briefly entered the outer world
during the Civil War: the Earl of Derby sided
with the Royalists and his Manx subjects
supported him by taking on the Republican English
Navy. The Manx were routed and their sea captain
Illiam Dhone suffered the ignominy of hanging at
his own yard-arm. The Earl of Derby was executed
by Cromwell in 1651. The Radcliffe family
remained on the island and the name survives to
this day. Also to this day survives the view in
Lancashire that Shakespeare spent years in the
county hiding behind the name of Shakeshaft.
Lancashire's witch epidemic was ended by the
Pendle trials of 1612. The Manx support for their
Wise men and women was so strong that Tynwald was
unable to pass its medical registration Act until
1899.

FADES OUT

Copyright Paul Robertshaw 2013 -'THE MANX TEMPEST'